THE *first* CHAPTER
THEN
I LET GO

THE *first* CHAPTER

THEN
I LET GO

TOWANNA PRESSLEY

The First Chapter Then I Let Go
Copyright © 2021 by Towanna Pressley

ISBN: 978-0-578-32840-9

Published by: Towanna Pressley
Printed in the United States of America
Layout and Design: InSCRIBEd Inspiration, LLC.

DEDICATION

I dedicate this book to my **daughter Tiana Westbrook** and my **son Ty'Reece Marshall-Pressley**. Thanks for choosing me as your mom and giving me so many reasons to never give up. If it wasn't for you, I don't know where I would be. I truly mean that.

I love you.

ACKNOWLEDGEMENTS

The first person I want to acknowledge is GOD. I thank Him for loving me when I didn't love myself. Lord, thank you for covering me and bringing me through every storm. From childhood to adulthood, you have never left me. I would not have made it this far without you! Thank you for life and life more abundantly. Although I went through many dark times, I know you carried me. Thank you for allowing me to release this book.

Thanks to everyone who helped me with this project. I never, and I mean never, could have done it without you!

To those that have lived through trauma, abuse (mental, emotional, or physical), depression, self-doubt, hurt and pain, please never give up. There are too many that didn't make it. I love each and every one of you.

To every **man, woman, and child who has been a victim of any violating crime**, please never give up! Get closer to God, believe, and have faith. There is light at the end of the tunnel. Remember, it is not your fault.

Thank you to my **mother, Mayme Fleet**, for giving me life and being one of the strongest women I have ever known.

Thank you to the man who raised me as his own, **Bravette Fleet**. You first called me your daughter at the age of two, and I've been yours ever since. I love you Dad!

Aunt Marilyn, thanks for the sacrifices you made for me, I didn't realize how huge they were until I had to raise kids of my own. I haven't forgotten.

My perfect guardian angels, my **grandmothers Daisy Chennault, Christine Sutton** and **Betty Fleet** and **my Stepmom Nadine Knox**, thanks for your part in helping to raise me. I hope I've made y'all proud. I miss y'all and I pray that you are resting peacefully.

My **siblings Bravette** and **my brother in-law José, Saron Fleet, Jamal, and my sister in-law Simone, Rashada Bryan, Nate Thompson** and my **sister in-law Angie**. Because of you, I have high blood pressure (lol). I love you guys and remember I will always be the oldest!

My stepsisters **Stephaine, Tracy, and Kim**. You guys gave me the chance to be a kid and treated me as if we shared the same DNA and I will forever love you for that.

My **aunts Denise** (she was the frugal one), **Rodnea** (she brought the gold), **Lisa** (she was the confidante of my boyfriends, lol) and **Uncle Gilbert** (he let all the kids drive), thanks for the roles you played in my life.

Daisy's grands: Ronald, Andrew, Jordy, William, Anthony, Ragina and **Marcus**, being the OLDEST, I created a different, but special relationship with each of you. Love you guys.

My **aunt/cousin Patricia Pressley**, when I wanted to come over you never told me no. You treated me as if I was your own. I did whatever your girls. When one got in trouble we all got in trouble! I love you and thanks!

My cousins **Tara and Channell**, thanks for being my big sisters. The two of you thought you were my mom! You could do anything to me BUT let someone else try it, they wouldn't try again. And that **Nastasha** well!!!! She was just a mean softy. Hahaha. Love ya'll.

My **closest and dearest friends/family** that were there during most of my storms, thank you! Whether we talk every day, or I haven't talked to you in years, I want to thank you for the role you played in my life.

Tiana Minor, Edward Nelson, Angie C., Roschell Thompson, Tera Jones, Lisa

Williams, Danielle Banks, Christine Bennett, Rikki Brown, Meatha Saunders, Melinda Wright, Diane Mapp, Thelma McGill, Marcia Smith Devona Cottman, Curtina Arbee, Kim Woolfolk, D'Nae McLane, Lynette Bell, Tracey Johnson, Dena Pelzer, Stephanie Pelzer, Germilla Clarke, Liza Johnson, and Lolita – thank you.

A special "I love you," to all of my nieces and nephews + my Great Niece EDYN. My God children Lakeisha Marshall, Christian, Christopher Johnson, and Aaron Webster. I love you guys so much.

Steven Westbrook and Maurice Marshall, thank you for my biggest accomplishments to date, MY KIDS! Without you, there would be no them.

Lastly, Mrs. Tiffany, thank you for making one of my dreams come true! I could not have done it without you.

Finally loving MYSELF,
Towanna

INTRODUCTION

Give thanks in all circumstances.
1 Thessalonians 5:18 (NIV)

Have you ever looked back in your life and wondered, "How did I make it?" Growing up, I could not see this far! I never thought I would make it, but GOD had different plans for me. The things I prayed for are happening and that sometimes scares me.

Sometimes you find yourself in dark places and don't see your way out. What about the times when you ended up in those places as a child because of the choices the trusted adults in your life made? That's a harder question.

I have found that life is full of those times, but yet, we can find where God was working, guiding, and protecting us. Even in those tough times, God says, "I'm still singing over you. I'm still the God who is more than able." People fail us, but God doesn't fail us.

Many studies show that people who are thankful and operate in gratitude are less likely to deal with envy or live in bitterness or resentment. These same people also usually have great blood pressure and sleep well. I pray that this book reminds you to give God glory in spite of your circumstances. Know that your present circumstance is not final. God can redeem you. God can change your life for the better. Be encouraged, better days are coming!

I want to put an end to generational curses. Molestation should not be the norm in families, nor should we remain silent. Silence destroys lives. Speak Up! Please, expose family secrets. Stop protecting pedophiles. Hurt people hurt people! It is time to change.

Keep Pressing,
Towanna

THE *first* CHAPTER
THEN
I LET GO

Contents

Chapter 1

The Beginning

On April 2, 1972, Easter Sunday, my mom, Mayme Pressley, a sixteen-year-old, was sitting on the couch when she started feeling sharp pains in her stomach. She screamed loudly and my paternal grandmother ran into the living room to see what was wrong. She explained that her stomach was hurting. My Grandmother called the doctor who advised that she take her straight to the hospital. When they got there, the doctors said she was not quite ready to deliver, but close enough that she could not go back home.

My mother and grandmother walked the halls for hours. In the early morning of April 3, 1972, with only my paternal grandmother by her side, my mother birthed me.

My name is Towanna Pressley. I was born at the Hospital of the University of Penn in Philadelphia, Pennsylvania. My first year of life was spent with my mom and the man named on my birth certificate as my "father."

At one point we lived in the Wynnefield section of Philadelphia. Back then it was one of the better areas of Philly. One day my mom was taking me for a walk in my stroller on 54th Street. A man followed us, trying to talk to her but she ignored him. The man on my birth certificate was following us from a distance and saw what was going on. He kidnapped the man and took him back to the apartment he shared with my mom and beat him, badly!

No one knew that the victim's father was f the head of law enforcement. He went and got his dad and cops raided the apartment. During the raid they found guns and drugs. Somehow I ended up on the floor during the raid. This is just one example of the type of things he would do . The man named as my "father" was a violent, aggressive person. He was well-known around town and feared .

He would often assault men and women. I always felt that my grandparents were afraid of him but accepted his behavior because he was their only child.

After that incident, my mother decided to leave. With the help of my paternal grandmother, she found an apartment on 52nd and Whitby Ave. This apartment was exactly five blocks from my maternal grandmother's house on 57th and Whitby Ave.

My aunt Marilyn told me how she used to walk to the apartment and my parents sometimes would be out of it. She said she would take me out to my grandmother's house and keep me for hours. I've been told sometimes they didn't even realize I had been gone! I was traumatized in early childhood.

Aunt Marilyn is my grandmother's third child. I used to visit her when she was in college. Aunt Marilyn and her friends spoiled me rotten like I was the daughter she never had. I went on dates with her and when I was a brat she canceled some of those dates.

She was one of the people who pushed me to do better! I remember studying for a spelling test and I was getting frustrated because she my aunt making rewrite the same things. You can't imagine how happy I was when I passed that spelling test.

When I was around seventeen, Aunt Marilyn gave birth to her first son, and he became my baby. I was the first grandchild for several years, so I received lots of attention.

Trauma

Although I received attention and love from my aunt and some of my other relatives, my childhood had several instances of trauma. Sometimes we use the word trauma, and don't fully understand the impact it can have on our life. What is trauma?

How can it affect your memory?

Trauma is an emotional response to a terrible event like an accident, rape, or natural disaster. Immediately after the event(s), shock and denial are typical. Longer term reactions include unpredictable emotions, flashbacks, strained relationships and even physical symptoms like headaches or nausea. (American Psychological Association, 2021) These things can, and do affect your memory. I experienced most of these situations in my life.

Your life can be impacted when you are born into trauma. A way that our bodies respond sometimes is to block out pain. I was born into a situation where I didn't have a consistent home environment and my mother later became a substance abuser. That was enough to cause trauma induced emotional coping skills to develop.

To this day I don't know how to swim, and never learned how to jump rope. I was called a dolly. Basically someone who could never take their turn jumping, so I would just turn the rope because I didn't know how to jump. Pretty sad. I was robbed of the opportunity to enjoy being a little girl and just playing. The bulk of my memories are taking care of myself and my siblings.

I believe that from my mother's womb, the devil tried to prevent me from becoming who God wanted me to be. One thing I know is that Satan will try to use your childhood issues to discredit the call of God on your life! After about seven or eight years old, nothing seemed "normal" about my childhood. I started to become more aware of my family's dysfunctional attributes. Things were always changing daily for me, and I was forced to continue to adjust to my environment.

I started to encounter pain. I started to feel misplaced. I was a young girl with my identity scattered and broken. There are many unanswered questions. I realized early that I had to set up a protective barrier for my heart, to keep people at a distance. I learned not to trust most people and always felt the need to keep "watching" people and their intentions even after I got to know them. I'm sure many of you can relate to that protective mechanism.

I have questioned and longed for answers. Some answers I have received and some I will never know. I lived in rejection and abandonment from my parents for most of my life. I know now that even though I felt alone at times, there are other children (who are now adults) that have gone through the same thing. The early stages of my life felt empty. I always felt that I didn't have the bond with a parent that a person is " supposed" to have.

I always felt like if the person whose egg was fertilized and the one whose sperm was used to create me couldn't love me or take care of me then I must not have been good enough! My mother was physically in and out of my life. I constantly felt isolated, alone, scared, and extremely vulnerable!

Interestingly enough, my life was in the hands of someone who needed care just as much as I did. It's hard to understand these kinds of things when you are young. Sadly my mother was molested at the age of 8 by her step-father and put out of the house at the age of twelve. I never could understand how a mother could put her daughter out on the streets. Many times I imagined my kids at twelve and not being able to think of anything that would make me put them out.

Over the years I have heard so many wonderful stories about my mothers' step-father. It was instilled in my brain that he was a great guy. They say that I cried when he passed because I didn't know who I was going to get an Easter Basket from anymore. This was my vision pretty much my entire life. As an adult I found out that he was a mean person.

On the flip side, some of the stories I've been told are that he was abusive to my grandmother, giving her black eyes often. He cheated and had an outside family. His inappropriate behavior did not end with my mother. He treated my great-great mother badly as well. He beat on kids that were not his. I heard there was nobody like him.

Now that I am an adult and have this information my opinion is that my grandmother was afraid of him, there is a huge chance that maybe she did know what was happening to my mother but was afraid to say anything. Back in those days the man was the head of the house and what they said went and if you spoke about what was going on inside your home you risked getting in lots of trouble. But he was not pleasant to be around.

To be honest if I had to pick between an Easter Basket and my Mother, my mother would win hands down. Being a victim myself I understand the impact and turmoil it can have on a person and even worse in a child. So I believe that if she was not robbed of her innocence, especially so young then maybe my life would have been better. No, I'm not saying that the situation is completely to blame but I do believe it was a start.

She got pregnant with me at fifteen and gave birth at sixteen. She wanted me so badly was so that she could have someone to love her unconditionally, which was the identical reason I had, when I gave birth to my first child. But what I learned is that you have to love yourself first, if not, it's impossible to love anyone else! Have you ever asked yourself why you have the parents that you have? If you have asked yourself that question ,you are not alone. We can't control the families that we are born into, but we can, with the work of the Holy Spirit, change our future.

I want to encourage you that you don't have to stay depressed about your past and your childhood! Yes, you went through it, but you don't have to stay there. There is hope for you. God wants to give you hope and a future. A future that is big and bright. A future that is bigger than you can imagine. But first, you must release the pain! God wants to heal you of your pain and your trauma. He wants to heal your heart!

"Cast all your cares upon him,
because he cares for us."
I Peter 5:7

I know a lot of times kids are taught not to show emotion, especially in the Black community. We were raised to be tough! If we did show emotion, we couldn't stay in that emotional place long or we would be looked at as weak. God actually gives us permission to give it to Him. The scripture 1 Peter 5:7 speaks volumes because to cast literally means to throw! So it's okay to throw your problems to God. He can handle it!

Pause For Reflection

Take this time to write down your trauma from your past or childhood that you need healed, so that you can be free!

_____

_____

_____

_____

_____

_____

_____

_____

_____

_____

_____

_____

_____

_____

Now that you written it out, believe that God is healing you from the hurt! It's time for you to laugh and smile again. Be free! Walk in freedom today.

Declare it with me today:

I am free to laugh.
I am free to smile.
I am free to sleep.
I am free to dream.
I am free to breathe.
I am free to love.
I am free to LIVE again.

Chapter 2

Childhood

When I was growing up, my grandmother's sister lived in Baltimore, Maryland and we would visit her sometimes. During one visit after I was born, she met a handsome man named Bravette. We spent most of that visit with him. My mother really liked him, he wasn't mean or abusive like my alleged "father" Furney.

After that visit was over we returned back to Philly. Furney would soon start beating on my mom again. I don't know exactly what happened after that or how it happened, but Bravette came to take us back to Baltimore.

When I was three, my mom and Bravette were married. We were now Baltimore residents, I lived there until around eleven years old. My step-father always treated me like his own flesh and blood and made sure he always showed me love. I genuinely felt like I was his daughter. My stepfather is my brother Bravette's and sister Saron's biological father, but he treated me so much better than even the one that was supposed to love me and supposedly "my dad." Sadly, my mother and father (Bravette) separated when I was five or six years old.

I was forced to "grow up early" as they say. I didn't get to enjoy being a child. I was responsible for my younger siblings and to be quite honest, I had to practically raise them for a period of time. My mother worked a lot, but she also ran the streets. So it was often me who would have to be home alone to take on the responsibilities of the household. Most of the times my mom was working and the other times she was out living her life.

Most of my days consisted of getting myself and my siblings ready for school and cooking dinner. Not to mention homework, baths and all the other things. I should have been having fun, but I remember always worrying about adult matters. School became a blur to me! I was going because I had too, not because I wanted to.

There is only one teacher I remember from my twelve years in school. Her name was Ms. Rabb and I believe she taught 3rd grade. I'm not sure why I remember her, but I do. I don't remember her face or what the classroom looked like. I just remember her name. I feel as if she was a person that truly cared about me and treated me nice. I don't get bad vibes when I think about her, but I also feel that there is a reason I remember her. It seems that school memories are fuzzy to me, but I have good memories of her.

I remember a lady and her daughter who fed us breakfast some mornings because her daughter and I walked to school together.

I would be so glad to have a hot meal and someone to feed us and having someone to at least walk to school with. It would have been nice to have memories of sitting with my mom every day before school and having breakfast, but that is not the case. One of the meals she gave us was round sausage on white bread with yellow mustard. It meant a lot to me, and I still eat that to this day, same brand of sausage and all.

During this part of my childhood, we had another aunt living in Baltimore. She was my Aunt Linda(she and my mother shared the same father). She had Tasha and George. There were times that we all lived together in the same house, so we all created special bonds with each other. When we didn't live together we still found time to spend with each other.

In addition to the responsibilities I had taken on at home, I also remember moving all the time! I moved back and forth between different houses. Nothing ever felt stable to me. The first time I ever felt stability in years was when I moved in with my step-father.

My mom eventually moved back to Philly with my brother and sister. One night while I was in the basement at my step-father's house the doorbell rang. My mom came to get me to take me back to live with her. I was mad about it! Like why would you take me away from my dad? I just couldn't understand and I didn't want to understand it. I didn't want to go back with her. And to make matters worse when I went to get in the car there was I believe both of my grandparents, the man on my birth certificate, my sister Saron and both of my brothers Jamal and Bravette. I always felt that my mother brought him (Furney) to try to intimidate my stepdad.

I didn't have a meaningful "relationship" with the man on my birth certificate (Furney) who was supposed to be my father, so I felt totally abandoned when she wanted to remove me from the only stable father that I knew.

I remember crying because I didn't want to leave. I remember my step-father crying with me and telling me that there was nothing he could do. I was so sad that day! A child shouldn't have to feel torn between parents, but I was! There was nothing we could do.

Did you ever have a time in your life where you felt torn between your parents? It's a terrible feeling. Statistics show that roughly one in two children will see their parents' divorce. 21% of children are being raised without fathers in the home in America.

Pause For Reflection

What was your family dynamic like growing up? Did you have both parents? Have you ever been separated from one of your parents? Did they divorce? How did it make you feel?

_____

_____

_____

_____

_____

_____

_____

_____

_____

_____

_____

_____

_____

If your parents separated or divorced when you were a kid, know that it wasn't your fault and it's still possible to heal from it and be able to move forward.

As I continue to reflect, I realized that I was taken back to Philly against my wishes, and once again I felt like I had to deal with things on my own. I also think that around that time I started to deal with anger and depression. A lot of my pre-teen years of living with my mother I have unfortunately blocked out but my 9th grade year, when I was about 14 sticks out to me the most!

My mom's behavior at this time kept changing drastically and she was still gone a lot! I did my best to make friends at school and that helped to keep my mind off of home life. But it was still very difficult for me.

I had a really good friend in high school named Angie. She would come to my house in the morning, and we would go to school together. As we got closer, Angie used to always wonder why I never wanted to go home. She said I would want to get off the bus as far away as possible and walk. I never really told her what was going on at home, however she does recall one time being at my house and watching my mom slap me in the face. Sad to say I don't even remember this. She said my mother slapped me so hard she was scared and went home. I had gotten so close to her.

Every day I wanted to be around her. As time went on I was a little traumatized because one day she was in school, and I kid you not the next thing I know she disappeared! I never knew where she was or where she went. I was really sad. All these years I have wondered where she went and what happened to her. In 2021 we were reunited after 35 years.

One of my fondest memories of High School was when there was a talent show at school. Salt and Pepper was one of the popular female rap groups at that time. A group of us decided to enter. I was Salt, Thelma was Pepper, D'Nae, and Curtina were our back up dancers, and Keith was our Herbie Love . We also had a DJ. We all had clothes that perfectly matched their clothes in the video. We practiced until we couldn't practice anymore.

Finally, the day of the show was here. I was really nervous at the last second and I didn't want to go on stage, but Curtina was the loudest one in the group, and she told me " oh you are going out there because we worked too hard." We did all the moves from salt n pepper and everything haha. And we made it through the performance, and we came in first place! Funny thing is, some of us just got together for a reunion recently and we were able to reminisce and laugh about it! I have a positive memory of graduation day in June 1990. Crack addiction and all ,my mother showed up to see me walk down that aisle. That made my day.

Growing up I had two special cousins that treated me like sisters. Channell was one of them. She is my step-father's niece. The moment my mother met my stepdad, I was his daughter, and his family was my family. We used to spend time together often. Channell knew that I was shy. When we were younger I was the good kid, and she was the terror. LOL! She would try to get me to lie for her, but I never would! We always found a way to make light of every situation we found ourselves in. She always made me laugh and had my back.

Before Rickey Smiley became a celebrity, he used to have fashion shows in Baltimore and she and I would be in them. All these events happened somewhere between 1975 and 1984-85. Channell was honestly more like a big sister to me. I remember she would try to boss me around, but she also protected me as well. Nobody could mess with me! Nobody! She was another person in my life that I felt I received love from. And I love her to this day.

Then there was Tara who is my older cousin's daughter. We were raised as sisters. One of my grandmother's sisters passed away years ago. My grandmother helped raise her children. One of her daughters is Tara's mom. So I grew up calling Tara's mom "Aunt" instead of cousin.

We grew closer every summer and on holidays. My mother moved back to Philly in 1984. Not long after I arrived in Philly, Tara and I were bonded like glue.

I would spend so many nights at her house that people thought I lived with them. For a while it was just Tara's mom, me, Tara, and her younger sister. It was spending time with Tara that I was the happiest.

The years get fuzzy between 1984 and 1987. My aunt moved into a house, and I went right along with them. Haha. BUT then, my aunt got married. So now it's my aunt, myself, Tara, her younger sister, and my aunt's husband. I was still very happy. Tara took Channell's role.

Tara and I did a lot together including juvenile jail time! Back in the 1980's there was a popular brand called Swatch. They had watches, bags, and other items. One day we went into the department store downtown called Strawbridge & Clothier and I took some clear pouches and got caught. We ended up in juvenile detention.

My great-uncle (my grandmother's brother) was the head of the juvenile detention center. To be honest we really weren't taking it seriously at first because we thought we were getting ready to go home. Tara's mom found out we were in there and my grandmother did too. Tara's mom wanted to come and get us, but my grandmother was like no leave them in there. She wanted to teach us a lesson.

We ended up spending the night there and that next morning, we heard my uncle's voice as he was walking near the cell we were in. The second we heard his voice, we just felt so much fear in that moment and knew we were probably in trouble! He never said anything, but I think that was a part of his scare tactic and a part of our punishment. He was the uncle in the family that many were afraid of and didn't like but he was one of my favorite uncles. He gave me the name "Dirty Reds". I don't remember exactly what happened after that but eventually we were released and were able to go home. It was only twenty-four hours, but I knew I never wanted to experience that again. It was something very immature I did because we both had more than enough money in our pockets to pay for it.

Tara was like a big sister always protected me. I always wanted to be around her. I remember spending the night and Tara wasn't in the room. Her stepfather touched me sexually while I was asleep. It made me uncomfortable, and I didn't know what to do. Being at their house was comforting to me. When her step-father started molesting me I said, and I did nothing. I loved Tara so much that although I knew it was wrong I didn't want anyone to tell me that I could no longer go to her house.

I never spoke of it to anyone! Not even to Tara. I wish I would have because maybe it would have put a stop to it but now we will never know. After it happened I blocked it out in my mind. I wanted to erase the pain. That is when I learned how to numb things and move past them. There are many things that victims of sexual violation deal with as a part of the aftermath of things like this. I hate when I hear people victim shaming:

- Why did she/he wait so long?
- She/He must want money.
- She's/He's lying.
- She/He wanted it.
- I just don't believe it.
- I don't care what they say my ___would never do that. (husband, brother, father, mother, aunt, uncle)

I did not have the courage to speak my truth until I was thirty-four. I woke up one day and said NO MORE. Sadly my grandmother had passed so I was never able to tell her what her son (Furney) did to me. I was able to talk to my aunt. I didn't know what to expect, I just knew that I needed to get it out. After I pushed the words out of my mouth and her heart returned back to normal, she grabbed and hugged me. We cried and I felt better once she let me go. A ton of bricks was lifted off of me. That's the day the healing process of my life started.

Pause For Reflection

What have you blocked out in your life? Were you molested, or raped? How have you coped? Have you sought counseling? Did you tell anyone? Have you released it? If you haven't released it, now is the time. Write out your feelings. Be free.

_____

_____

_____

_____

_____

_____

_____

_____

_____

_____

_____

_____

Reflections About my Brother

I can't talk about childhood memories and not talk about my younger brother. We have the same mother. I am four years older than him, he's the middle child. My brother remembers that I was responsible for them. He remembers being between the ages of four and eight-years-old and me taking on adult responsibilities by caring for him. I did my best to figure out how to nurture him. I wanted to be there for him as much as I could and was fond of him.

Although we were alone often, we had family within a block. Our great aunt would check on us, because she lived around the corner from us. I know that my brother has painful memories too, because he was even younger, and he would see that our mom would just go ghost and sometimes for days at a time. Sometimes she was working, other times she was just running the streets!

I know that took a toll on him. I vaguely remember a period of time where he and my sister were separated from me. I was sad and devastated and I didn't understand why. I wanted us to all be together and to just be stable. But it never seemed possible.

I have a different dad than Bravette and Saron. As far as our fathers, my father lived in Philly and their father lived in Maryland.

There was a time that my mom was dating a guy and they would get in fights all the time! So Bravette, my sister and I witnessed a lot of verbal and physical abuse in the home too. I remember my mother and her boyfriend fighting one day and me and Saron started beating him with a curtain rod!

One day, when Bravette was, I believe in 6th or 7th grade, my mom and this guy she was dating at the time moved to Philly. We moved in with this guy's family and that guy, (my mother's boyfriend) molested Bravette! I didn't know that this was happening. I later found out when we were older. I won't get into all of those details, but I often wonder how many more of us in the family have been molested and have kept silent about it.

Things were moving fast around that time and still a blur but all I know is that one day, our dad picked Bravette and Saron up from school, and then came to the house with the police! I'm not sure why but I assume he had some type of court papers because he took Bravette and Saron back to Baltimore with him.

Eventually my mom went into deeper depression and her drug abuse spiraled out of control. As Bravette got older he would express himself in different ways, some good and some bad. But I know he loved me as his sister. I always played the mother role for him, and he has expressed how he appreciated me for that.

I remember when he started a singing group today known as Dru Hill and my step-dad was not having it because school was more important to him. He was invited to the Apollo and came in first place that year.

As his big sister, I was the only one that he called after he won. I was always very supportive of him and still am. But not just him. I have always had to be there for everybody. I was a strong kid and strong young lady. Seriously. I have come to realize that now and sadly, I shouldn't have had to be so strong, being so young but I had no choice.

Pause For Reflection

Was there a point in your childhood where you felt forced to be strong? Was there a time when you just wanted to be a kid? God sees you and he knows. It's okay to breathe and release it. I'm so glad that I did, and you will be too! You can write about it here.

_____

_____

_____

_____

_____

_____

_____

_____

_____

_____

_____

_____

Did you release it?

Chapter 3

Navigating Through Life

During my childhood, I encountered so many different dysfunctional things that I lost count of them. Life was rough.

The impact of not having a mother to actually raise you can cause severe trauma, depression, and other mental health disorders. Growing up I can't even begin to describe to you the sadness I felt at times.

My mother wasn't able to help me through hormonal and body changes. She wasn't there for things I had going on at school, or when I started liking, and dating boys in high school. She missed when I had my first heartbreak.

I should have been able to ask my mom what to do or ask her for comfort but of course I didn't know where she was and that memory sticks out so strongly in my mind so I know that it must have been traumatic for me.

My mother was always doing her thing. Some of the time she was working or doing homework other times God only knows. As I got to my pre-teen years, right before high school is when I believe her addiction started. At this time she had lost custody of my siblings, so it was just me. All she ever wanted was to be a nurse and get my siblings back.

When she was younger she would tell me how she would rescue different types of animals, nurse them back to health and let them go. She just loved helping and wanted to be loved herself. Eventually the stress, depression, and pressure of losing her kids and nursing school became overwhelming. She just wanted the pain to go away. She said that one day one of her white classmates introduced her to a white powder. This white powder was supposed to help her concentrate and stay up long enough to get her work done. I don't think there's much to say after that.

I often wonder what it would have been like to be able to just have her to guide me in life and give me wisdom and help me to figure things out. It would have been great to have her hug me often and for her to tell me that she loved me or how beautiful I was to her. It would have been nice to just have times where we did girlie things together. Although she had her flaws she was a very glamorous mother, and always put herself together well and gave us a nice home with nice things. She always made sure that we had food in the house, clothes and that our utilities were never off. She would make sure that we were taken care of to the best of her ability. She is one of the only people I know that can literally turn trash to treasure.

Everything else was on me. I had to be the woman of the house, as a little girl still and I really didn't know how but every year that went by, and I made it through, it felt like I accomplished something. I felt that I did the best I could.

As a child I felt frustrated, and stuck. But there was nothing I could do about the circumstances except to deal with them. Even though around this time I didn't really look forward to it a whole lot, but I did enjoy spending time with my friends. When I was between the ages of seven and ten, I remember spending a lot of time with a girl named Danielle. My cousin Vanessa was engaged to her uncle, and we instantly started calling each other cousins.

We had so much fun together in the house! My brother used to be home too and always wanted to be around us! It seemed like it was every second. I have to admit, I was pretty tough on him and found myself always saying "Get out of my room!" or "Go do your homework!" I really just wanted to play with Danielle by myself.

My mother used to have this super tv and that was like our cable back then. Oh, and a jukebox! We used to love to watch music videos of New Edition and Run DMC. We used to sneak and try to watch dirty movies which we had no business doing. I always found myself getting in trouble with Danielle.

Boys started liking me around that time. And whenever Danielle was at my house, I would make them like her too! Haha. We were so bold, we used to flash the boys that we liked outside my bedroom window. The boys used to tell Danielle to come closer because she was darker than me so they couldn't see her as well as they could see me, haha!

We thought that the only reason they liked us was because we had been showing them our boobs but one day they confirmed that they really did like us for our personalities and actually wanted us to be their girlfriends.

At the time she and I liked the same boy, so we said no to their offer. My mom had been working a lot, so she wasn't home when we were talking to boys, so we thought we were in the clear! Haahaha.

Later on that next week, one of the neighbors came over and told my mom what we had been doing. She told her we were being fast and flashing boys. Whew. We got in so much trouble. Danielle couldn't come over to the house for a while. We both were both on punishment. But thankfully, we still saw each other at school.

There was a girl named Tia Cooley that used to bully me in elementary school. I didn't like fighting and had never been in many fights, but Danielle would make me. I would get in fights with the girl bullying me. I can say she probably won the first couple fights. But one day I was sick of it, and I decided to really fight back. All I will say is that she never bullied me again. Apparently, she and I were the only light skinned girls at school and that's why she didn't like me.

I never started fights but other kids didn't like me and would always start trouble with me or start a fight with me. I would get mad when Danielle didn't jump in to help me. She finally told me , "Look, don't pull hair, you have to punch them!" I got in a couple more fights after that, I tore a couple girls up and I won the fights. I was happy because Danielle didn't have to jump in my fights anymore. The girls never messed with me again unless I was by myself, so Danielle and I confronted them again about it, and they finally left me alone.

Looking back I'm so appreciative of Danielle. I think we all had that one friend in school that would tear somebody up about you and would be down for whatever at any time. She was that for me.

As time went on, some of my most vivid memories are the ones that I shared with my best friend, Tiana.

Tiana and I had been best friends since we were teenagers. I can remember meeting her when we were fourteen at Philly's work-ready program for teens. We both wanted to be hair stylists, so we were in the cosmetology program together. It taught us absolutely nothing about cosmetology. We had more fun than we had work to actually do.

I mentioned that I loved her name and that if I ever had a daughter I was going to name her Tiana. Unfortunately, we lost touch after the end of the program. I can remember writing her a letter and her being surprised and us talking and losing touch again.

Several years later , we ran into each other at the laundromat on 53rd and Baltimore Ave. I was so happy to see her. As we were talking to each other, my daughter walked up, and I mentioned to Tiana that she was my daughter. I remember at that moment I asked her "what did she think her name was?" and then I said Tiana. She was so happy and honored that I remembered saying it five years prior and that I actually did what I said I was going to do.

It didn't take long for our friendship to pick up where we left off. But as they say "The devil is busy " Tiana and I were spending a lot of time together catching up on everything that we missed over the years. Soon after the nightmare began.

Tiana had been dating a guy named Mitchell for approximately two years. We later found out that he was seeing another woman. Upon the completion of our investigation, the other woman was revealed. The other woman was a close friend of mine from high school. I hated the position I was in… My best friend and my close friend were dating the same guy. Tiana was a homebody and was not too fond of partying and being in the mix, however; my close friend enjoyed hanging out. A few weeks passed after the exposure and Tiana expressed her distaste for the situation. She was upset with me and did not want me to associate myself with the other woman anymore. Tiana was conflicted but chose to stay around to learn more about what was going on.

I can remember, one day Tiana was walking down the street and we pulled up in the car!

When we both pulled up, the girl started asking Tiana questions about Mitchell. I can recall that Tiana just stood there looking at me in disbelief. I didn't say anything at the time and I'm not sure why. It was a very uncomfortable position to be in.

Tiana and I did some crazy things. I liked this guy that we will call KC. I really liked him. He lived in the Spring Garden area of Philadelphia. We would often ride past his house. One day we were riding pass and KC was coming out the door. We thought he saw us, so we stopped. We talked to him for a few then pulled off. We laughed so hard we almost peed our pants because we got caught. We have sat outside of people's houses, in the middle of basketball courts in the middle of the night and all different types of things. We were like Thelma and Louise.

Tiana and I enjoyed life in different ways as our personalities are unique. I was the more outgoing counterpart. Tiana was a little shy and did not converse with as many people as I did. I remember having a sex demonstration party on behalf of Tiana. She had the desire, ideas, everything except one thing - THE PEOPLE (lol). We were grown and as our elders would say, "smelling ourselves" so we were convinced that we could do it, and we did. Tiana was the yin to my yang! Our unique personalities allowed us to sometimes live vicariously through each other.

Tiana and I used to have so much fun. One of my most positive memories of our friendship was when I got baptized.

Tiana was actually there for me. She witnessed the entire service. It was such a special day and I remember feeling happy that day. It was beautiful and Tiana still has the pictures! The only thing that was noticeable and affected how I felt around that time was my teeth, especially in pictures.

As time went on, I decided that I wanted to straighten my teeth out. I was so excited about getting braces. Tiana was happy for me too!

Tiana and I shared some amazing memories that will last us a lifetime. One day she called me upset, crying hysterically - she was devastated. She had received some debilitating information that could have potentially changed the course of her life and it terrified the both of us. You could not tell my bestie that she wasn't dying. I later learned that my friend is the biggest hypochondriac I know (lol). What Tiana shared with me during that phone call is one of my fondest memories. Basically she thought she was dying. She asked me if I could raise her children if she didn't make it through because she thought I was an amazing mother. Her thoughts of my parenting pulled on every string in my heart. That was a defining moment in my life. Regardless of what I had been through, at that moment I was determined to supply my daughter with a better life and love than I previously knew.

To this day I'm still blown away by that and it still warmed my heart. I wasn't a perfect mother myself, but I was just so in awe that she would ask me such a thing. Regardless of how I feel about my life and things that may have happened that weren't the best between her and I, I would have done it in a heartbeat.

I knew then that no matter what happened in our lives that we would always be connected in some way and hopefully always find our way back to each other. As much as we had good times, we had some tough moments that we endured together too. For example, I remember nights where I don't know what I would have done without her.

During our early 20's I remember being out late at night with her knocking on crack house doors looking for my mom. One of the times we saw her, and she told the person who answered the door to tell me she wasn't there. That hurt me so badly. Now that I'm older I know that my mother avoided me only out of embarrassment and shame. What I wanted her to know is that I didn't care about any of that, I just wanted her to come home.

Yes, I know it was dangerous! Looking back, I shouldn't have been going to those places and involving Tiana either. But you couldn't tell me all that then. I would get such an adrenaline rush going up and down Erie

41

Ave. searching high and low for her! I missed her and got worried and just like any normal girl, I just wanted my mom even if she wasn't the best thing for me at the time. I wanted to be near her. I wanted to know if she was okay. I was so concerned about her. She was still my mom and I wanted to look for her. I still cared about her. Sometimes we wouldn't find her after what seemed like we searched for hours. I'll never forget those times with Tiana. Even though we were young adults, she really showed me what it was like to have somebody really try to be your friend. A real friend.

I started dating Donnell, = Tiana's brother. Tiana and I were blown away when he gave me raggedy drive-by flowers for Valentine's Day!! Haha. We were both pissed about it and cursed him out badly.

I stopped talking to Donnell after a while. Things didn't work out. Several years later I started talking to Pooge. Pooge is actually my son's father. I first started dating him around 16. Then again in 1998. We broke up and started dating again in 2003 and my son was born in August 2004.

I remember I was upset with him, because there was a time he "thought" I was out of town. I ended up finding out he had some type of party. The time frame was around February or March 2004 with God knows who in the house. At the time he was doing things that negatively affected his thought process and he made bad decisions. We eventually broke up for the final time.

Pause For Reflection

Have you ever had a time in your life where you were scared, and you felt like your life was on the line? Who did you lean on during that time? How did you feel? Did you give it to God or try to deal with it on your own? Take the next couple of pages to write it out, release it to God and don't pick it back up!

_____

_____

_____

_____

_____

_____

_____

_____

_____

_____

_____

_____

Chapter 4

Adulthood

Fast forwarding to our adult years. The year was 2001, I was in Philly and Bravette moved in with me.

Everything bad started happening with him and his music career and my brother was upset because he couldn't do everything that he wanted to do after he moved in with me. He was mad. He was acting like a fish out of water in Philly and we began to not get along. There was a lot of yelling and screaming in the home.

He says he remembers that I would blame him for everything in the house. That's not how I see it. I just wanted to help him out, but I wanted him to keep things clean and organized in my house. Everything such as paper plates not being used enough, too many dishes in the sink etc. He didn't want to deal with it. I got tired of this and so did he and eventually it put a big strain on the relationship we had.

I know it seems pretty petty now but at the time these things mattered most. I couldn't control a lot growing up so now the things that are within my control like in my home environment. Plus I believe in taking care of the things you have.

To be honest, I was dealing with a lot. My brother was also dealing with a lot as well and he started to get into things that he shouldn't have that I won't get all the way into, but he was just trying to survive.

So now, I can say things are better. We have come a long way as a family. My mother lives around the corner from me. She's a little better but her decision making is still lacking, and I believe that has affected my decision making as well over the years. Nevertheless, I have done my best to set new standards for myself as well as my children.

My brother moved out. Then a few years later Nan Nan came into play. Let me give a little of the backstory. On November 11, 1991, the man listed on my birth certificate had a baby girl. Between 1996 and 1998 he was given custody of my sister. In 2001 he passed away.

My grandmother was too old to raise her, so I went to the courts and gained custody of her. She was with me a year or two before she went to live with her mother. I actually was excited that she was coming to live with us.

Because she and my daughter were the same age I figured they could grow up more like sisters. They went to the same school and were on the same drill team. I felt safer knowing that they were at the same places so they could look out for one another. As time went on my sister would visit her mother on the weekends. It came to a point where I thought her mother had gotten herself together, so I let my sister go live with her. We had an agreement that she would keep in contact with me however, we didn't. I may have heard from her a few times in the beginning but then communication stopped. I would call but never got an answer.

After several attempts, I assumed maybe my sister didn't want to talk to me, so I stopped. I knew how I felt wanting to be with my mother, so I assumed that's what she was doing. We were estranged for about 15 years. We finally reconnected.

We drove to my grandparents' grave site to visit them. While we were there we also visited the man on my birth certificates grave as well. We sat there and talked for hours about everything. I never shared with her that I hated his grave site, and it didn't matter how many times I went to visit my grandparents I never walked twenty-five feet to visit him. That was my second time, the first was with my grandmother before she passed. Little did my sister know I sat there that long for her.

The short story is she was hurt and angry with me because she felt that I abandoned her but the whole time I felt as if she didn't want to be bothered with me. Had I known she would go through half of what she went though I would have never let her go. This is one of the downfalls of not having good communication. I had to forgive myself for that as well. I truly love my sister and hope one day she truly forgives me.

After my sister moved in with me that left my grandmother and grandfather still living in the house. In 2002, my grandfather passed, which left my grandmother alone.

There was a woman that my grandmother helped raise so she was considered family. My grandmother really had a lot of trust in her. My grandmother still looked at her grandchildren as kids, we didn't know much.

Shortly after my grandfather passed, this man named Tommy popped up on my grandmother's doorstep saying that he somehow was family. He said he was my grandmother's nephew. I never got a clear understanding of how he was related, I just knew I didn't like him!

The man on my birth certificate (Furney) lived with my grandmother until his death, he was the only child. So with her husband and son both gone her health started to deteriorate. I believe my grandmother felt that men were superior because when Tommy showed up she instantly trusted and believed everything he had to say.

His opinions overrode everyone's including the woman she trusted so much. At this time, the woman still was involved with my grandmother's finances. My grandmother's "things" would soon become the main topic between the woman and this man Tommy. My grandmother went to stay with the woman, and I was shocked.

Tommy would call to check on my grandmother often. He asked the woman if he could take my grandmother to New Jersey for a few days. If I'm not mistaken she didn't want him too, but my grandmother heard and understood what was going on and said that she wanted to go. They left. When it was time to return her he refused to bring her back. Now what in the world?!

The woman contacted a lawyer. The lawyer started by saying he would petition the court to have my grandmother removed from Tommy's care. Sadly, she was placed in some type of nursing home. The lawyer said that because she was taken out of state that the case wouldn't be that easy. I remember my mother and I, going to visit her and taking her to IHop.

When it was time to take her back she said that she did not want to go. Of course I didn't want to leave her, but the courts stated that we had to. I just promised her that she would not be there long. The woman and I were cordial with each other but never close. I knew that she hired a lawyer, but she never gave me any real details about what exactly was going on, but I do know that Tommy had already told the courts that she was not biologically related.

This became a big issue with the judge. The judge wanted to talk to a person related to my grandmother. At that point the woman decided to include me. Thank God! It wasn't because she wanted to but because I was the only relative she could use.

I went along with it because I wanted to know what was going on. The first court date was in Jersey. My memory gets a little foggy at this point. But I know after that first court date, that I didn't have custody of my grandmother.

While dealing with this I found out I'm pregnant. At first thought I said this baby got to go! During this time I couldn't imagine myself with any more children. Because at the time I always only wanted one child and I wanted a girl, and I already had my girl, so I was good. Plus having another little person calling me mommy was very scary.

Imagine feeling like you have all you need then BOOM you are pregnant by a man that is stressing you out. I just didn't want another baby. I was sad and depressed because of what I was already going through in the relationship with him. I was saying to myself, "God, I don't want no baby! "So one day, I called the abortion clinic and I set up the appointment.

I went to sleep, and I know it's going to sound crazy, but I ended up having this very mind boggling dream! In this dream, I got the abortion, but I died, and I somehow was in heaven and there were babies running after me and yelling at me saying " why you kill me, why did you kill me?" I woke up scared to death! I decided not to have the abortion.

A few weeks later, my unborn son's father and I were arguing. And so I had decided I didn't want to sleep in the bed with him. I slept downstairs on the couch snuggled up in my tan comforter with green flowers on it.

At the time I had cream furniture. Still trying to wrap my mind around having another baby, I will never forget that I woke up and my comforter was no longer tan, but it had blood all over it and my cream sofa was completely saturated in blood. I was so scared. And to be honest, I already talked to God about this, but I was sitting there saying to myself, welp God knew I wasn't ready for another baby, so he took the stress, pressure, and guilt of even having the thought away.

I assumed I had a miscarriage, so I cleaned myself and everything up and I proceeded to go on with my life and to put that behind me, So I thought! A few days later, I'm still not feeling right. So I made an appointment for a couple days later. I went to the doctor, and I was sitting in the exam room, and they ran all kinds of tests to see what was going on. I was waiting for them to come back in to see me.

The nurse came back to see me, she closed the door, and said "Congratulations!"

I said, "Congratulations for what lady?!!"

The nurse responded, "You're pregnant!"

I was in utter shock and disbelief! I proceeded to tell her that there was no way that I could be pregnant! I began to tell her the story of what happened with the bleeding I had the week prior.

They decided to take additional blood work and figured out that my HCG levels were pretty high. They did an ultrasound and realized that I had been pregnant with twins! The bleeding was the result of me miscarrying one. I was devastated. It was bittersweet because my son was in my womb and thriving.

Months went by and it was finally time for me to have my son. I went into labor and had him. He was born August 23, 2004. I'll never forget the pain that I felt that day. Those pains were totally different from 1991 when I gave birth to my daughter. The day I had my son ,my mother, brother, daughter, and neighbor were in the delivery room with me while my aunt and little cousin sat in the visiting room. I was yelling so loud they could hear me!

My son's heart rate was low, so they had to rush me in for an emergency c-section. Prior to going to the hospital, I walked to the corner store to get a roast beef and cheese hoagie. The pains had started but weren't too bad so I thought a little walk would help. It took me forty minutes to walk. By the time I got back I no longer wanted the hoagie. I then started walking up and down in my backyard because that fast the pains were starting to be unbearable. My cousin Jordy was working for an ambulance company at the time and so happened to stop to visit. His visit turned into me being placed in his ambulance and taken to the hospital.

I finally was able to eat and get some sleep after he was born. I look up and who do I see? My son's father shows up to the hospital drunk. Not only that he shows up with people that I don't even know. I was beyond mad but there wasn't much that I could do.

This was the first time I had seen him since we broke up months earlier. I'll never forget the day I came home to find out that he had a party in the house while I was gone. This party consisted of men, women, drugs, alcohol, and guns. There was a porno in my DVD player, red hair in my soap dish in the bathroom and some trifling female panties in my backyard. I'm assuming he made everyone jump the fence in the backyard and she dropped them. They even ate all the food I prepared before I left. Moments like that reminded me of why we weren't ever going to work out and I have no regrets of being done with him!

Although we broke up and that situation hurt me really badly, I could never hate him. I met Pooge when one of my closest sister/friends Lisa was dating his brother Keith. Pooge was straight from jail when we started dating, I was in high school.

She would be at their house all the time and I would want to be there with her. I remember one day walking to their house in the morning thinking I was going to play hooky from school. Boy was I wrong. Once he saw that I was there he gripped me up and didn't let go until I was in the passenger's seat of his car. He started driving and when the car came to a complete stop I was in front of my school.

He smiled and said "I will see you at 3:00. I was mad but just as he said he was there at 3:00, outside leaning on his car drinking out of a 64 oz Hi C juice can. He was a little older than me so he could have easily let me hooky school that day, but he didn't. That could have been an early start to becoming a high school dropout, but he wasn't going for it. Shopping in Atlantic City was the in thing back then. We would ride down to the shop often coming home with Gucci, MCM and Iceberg bags. I remember putting some earrings on lay-a-way. They were gold octagon shaped with gold rope around them with my name and a champagne glass on them.

A guy that liked me volunteered to get them out of layaway. When it was time for me to get my earrings he refused to give them to me unless I went to his house. I was pissed because I didn't like the fact that he was trying to hold my earrings hostage. I decided to tell Pooge who took me too his house, knocked on the door and brought back my earrings.

We had a lot of bad times, but we did share some good things. And for that I will always have a special spot in my heart for him. Did I mention my one and only god-daughter Lakeisha is his niece, Keith's daughter. She was my first baby. Our birthdays are a day apart. I remember praying that her mother went into labor on my birthday but of course she was a stubborn Aries from the start and came a day after. I spoiled her rotten.

I remember her mother trying to make her mad telling her that once I had my own baby that I would not love her anymore. She thought that was funny. I didn't. Haha. I think one way or another I spoiled all 4 of my god kids. Several years after she was born I welcomed my twin godsons Christain and Christopher. They sent me on wild goose chases looking for things they wanted every year, but it was exciting doing it. Lately there is Aaron. He's the youngest, that's my baby.

Nevertheless, I am so grateful for my son, and I am so glad to have him. He was made out of love, so I know that he was meant to be here. He changed my life! And I couldn't imagine life without him.

Back to my Nan Nan story! The second court date in Philadelphia was on January 3, 2005. Tommy was no longer involved. This hearing was to decide what was going to happen with my grandmother who was diagnosed with dementia.

The woman my grandmother trusted had all her paperwork and control of her finances. Supposedly, that was Tommy's reason for taking her. He told the courts that the woman was taking advantage of my grandmother! So on January 3, 2005, myself, the woman, and her daughter appeared in court.

The end result was the judge asking the woman, (since the finances were the issue) would she be willing to continue taking care of my grandmother but allowing me to have control over all finances? That would include me paying her for providing the care.

The woman immediately got upset and said "No!" She said that if I had to take control of her finances then I would have to take my grandmother as well. At this time I had a baby that was just 5 months old and a 13 year old daughter and I had just started a new job that I had only been working for two months but there was no way I could just abandon her. Not having a clue as to what I was going to do I told the judge that I would take responsibility for her. I left court with my grandmother.

The judge appointed me as her new caregiver, and I gained full custody of my paternal grandmother. When I left the courts, we went to my maternal grandmother's house. My maternal grandmother was living in a 4 bedroom house alone, so she agreed to take in my paternal grandmother for me.

My grandmother kept my (Paternal) grandmother from January 2005 until September 2006. She kept her for me on Sundays through Fridays. She also kept my newborn son because I started a new job. So every day I would get up early in the morning, drop off my son to my grandma and go to work. Then, I would come back to my grandmother's house, pick up my son and visit with my grandmother's and go back home and do the same thing all over again the next day. I was very tired. But I did this for a while. I did this for around eighteen months.

The agreement was I paid $900 to my grandma to do this for me. She was getting $500 a month for my son. I still liked to spend time with my grandma, so on Fridays I would pick up my grandma and my son , keep my grandma for the weekend, take care of her and my baby, do my grandmother's hair and then take her back to my other grandmother's house on Sunday night. This entire process lasted for almost two years. As time went on, my maternal grandmother started acting funny. She acted like she was starting to get annoyed

with keeping my grandmother. Family
members started gossiping and she started
treating me differently.

A little backstory:

There is a history between my
grandmothers. They lived directly across the
street from each other literally. One address
was 5325 and the other 5326. Story goes that
my maternal grandmother treated my mom
badly. My paternal grandmother met my
mother while my mother was dating her son.
My paternal grandmother's house was a safe
haven for my mother. Both have said a thing or
two about each other to me over the years but
never to the degree where I thought one didn't
like the other.

On September 6, 2006, the day after Labor
Day I went to drop my (Paternal) grandmother
off as usual. I got her ready for bed and went
to tell my (Maternal) grandmother that I was
leaving. She would usually say ok "good
night" but this night she said, "You better take
your grandmother with you". I responded by
saying "Huh" She repeated" You better take
your grandmother with you" I was stuck.

A few weeks prior she did tell me she wanted me to start making other plans in regards to my grandmother. I didn't understand where that came from so sudden because she didn't give an exact deadline. I said OK, walked back to the room my grandmother slept in, got her re-dressed her and took her home with me.

It was rumored that a few family members never wanted my grandmother to provide care for my grandmother from the beginning. I was a little frustrated because she let me get her ready for bed only to tell me to take her back with me and she knew I had to work. It's like she didn't care about me or that I had a job .

I started getting worried, because I needed to keep my job. I had no clue what I was going to do. All I knew was that I had to be at work at 8:00am the next morning.

I contacted my supervisor the next morning to explain to her what was going on. I was able to immediately use all my sick, personal and vacation days. When my grandmother told me to start making other plans, I immediately applied for FMLA at my job.

During this time, I would hear so many rumors about what if anything I was doing in regards to getting my grandmother. What they didn't know was that I was denied FMLA 4 different times. Because my grandmother wasn't my parent or child, FMLA was almost impossible to get. The process was so draining but after several appeals and right before all of my time was used up, I won the appeal. I could relax a little now to focus on what was next. Thankfully, I was able to get FMLA and I was able to use some of the time to look after her, but I was still mad.

My grandmother absolutely loved her house. She treasured her house so much, so I had decided that I wanted her last days to be in her house. The house needed renovations, so I had been working on the house and started trying to get it ready for her to be able to go back to living in it.

One day I decided to drive to her home to do some work and I brought her with me. She never forgot my name, but we were standing in front of her house, and I asked her do you know where we are? I was thinking she would be happy but instead she replied "no!" That was a hard moment for me when I actually started crying! It really hit me how bad the dementia was for her to be standing in front of the house that she once loved so much and not remembering it made me so sad.

At one point she was just yelling at me "Towanna please help me!" "I don't know where I am." This was heartbreaking for me to hear! After a while I was able to move my grandmother back into her own house and I hired a caregiver to look after my grandmother, but I told her she could stay there for free!

I paid her $500 for her pocket but she didn't have to worry about buying anything other than her personal stuff. I got everything set up with the caregiver and literally moved my grandmother into her house on Sunday and she passed away that next Sunday.

So, I always thanked the lady, because my goal for my grandmother's last days was to be in her house. And she was. However, I later found out that the lady had moved her son into the house!

So for a while I gave myself headaches wondering if something went wrong! Was the decision to move her back into her home a mistake? I had some unanswered questions and always felt bad, and I apologized to my grandma after she passed and still do.

I ended up evicting the lady from the house. I went over there, and the house wasn't clean. Then what made it so bad was, I went into the room where the lady had been sleeping. There were mouse turds in the bed where she used to sleep. I often felt guilty and wondered if it was too much for my grandma to witness and deal with.

I only have one regret and that is we didn't make it to the casino. NaNa loved the casino. I remember being a teenager and either going on a bus trip or driving to Atlantic City. Those were the days you could put loose change in the machines and kids could go in. At least I think they could because I would sit in the seat next to Nan Na and pull the handle. I would always win a little something.

I was trying to get over the hurt and pain from losing one grandmother, unaware that I would face that same pain again soon. Four months prior to my paternal grandmother passing I had written my maternal grandmother a check that was to cover September. I had written her the check in advance but when I had to take my grandmother back with me she had not taken care of her for September. I was still keeping my grandmother at that point, but I had paid her in advance.

So she basically had received the check, got paid, but she didn't work for it yet because that was the same night when she told me I was going to have to take my grandmother with me and that she wasn't keeping her for me anymore. So that money did not belong to her.

I had a conversation with her about not cashing the check because she hadn't worked for it. So, I assumed she got rid of the check and wasn't still holding on to it all that time.

But apparently, that wasn't the case. Well, after my paternal grandmother passed, literally the next business day I got an alert on my phone that the check had been cashed! I was really upset because my grandmother had just passed number one and number two, that wasn't her money to have because she hadn't earned it.

It had barely been twenty-four hours. I found out that of course it wasn't my grandmother (the one who I wrote the check to) that did it, but it was one of my aunt's that had cashed the check as if they were doing it for her.

I was livid. I just felt like that was really wrong and disrespectful. I just felt like that was mean and very evil spirited. It really hurt. Not so much the money but them taking it and cashing it. What kind of person would do that? It was basically like they were stealing from me and had no respect for my paternal grandmother's death either!

I was very angry. As a matter of fact I was so angry that I ended up suing my grandmother for the money back. My aunts and other family members started talking about me even more and saying, "I can't believe you are suing your own grandmother" and all this other stuff. Now the family was divided. I felt alone during that time. The family was against me. But I didn't care because it wasn't right. Some weeks went by, and we went to court. I pleaded my case to the judge anyway. At the end of the court hearing, I ended up winning.

The judge then asked me what I wanted to see happen. I told the judge that I didn't want the money back from my grandmother, but I wanted all the degrading of my name, and defamation of character to stop at the time because of what my family was putting me through. They knew it wasn't right because when they cashed it they conveniently waited until my other grandma passed.

So even though I won the case it was just for the principle of the matter. So I just eventually left it alone because the point had been made, and I received some type of justice!

In June 2009 my maternal grandmother passed, which is not too long after my paternal grandmother. I ended up finding out that my maternal grandmother had cancer. She was living with my aunt at the time , the one that I was barely talking to at the time either, the one that cashed the check.

I was pretty much completely estranged from my grandmother and my aunt and to be honest it really, really hurt. You know, that's my grandma. We were once very close and she played a vital role in raising me, both of them did. and they meant a lot to me.

I remember being called Mickey Mouse in High School because I wore a lot of Mickey Mouse styled clothes. It was actually the in thing back then. Even as an adult she was my safe haven. When my feelings were hurt or I didn't feel well , I used to lay in her bed. Just lying there gave me so much comfort.

I decided after hearing the news that I would put my big girl panties on and call my aunt and ask her if I could come to her house to see my grandmother! I had to humble myself. I was going through a lot of different emotions, and I had to deal with everything myself because it seemed like the world was mad at me. But yet and still, I humbled myself and called my aunt.

So, I went to go see her. She had a doctor's appointment, and we all went to the appointment. Soon after that she went back home, and she had to be under hospice care at her own home. At that point she wasn't at my aunt's anymore. They brought a special bed out for her. By this time, we all started taking turns and spending the night over to the house to be around her during her last days of battling the cancer.

As time went on , we spent as much time with her as we could. Her birthday was June 14th. I remember that we had a little party for her. She could barely talk around this time, and I remember some of her last moments, about a few days after her birthday when she was laying in the bed. We were at the house and some of her last words were "somebody tell Towanna to shut up!". Haha. That still sticks out in my mind. My grandmother always spoke her mind and she was subject to say anything!

After my grandmother passed, everyone started coming over and going through my grandmother's house looking for different things. And of course my aunt was there. My aunt's behavior towards me and my daughters' company the day my grandmother passed was just mind blowing! What was her behavior? Well, there was already tension in the family.

My aunt was upset with a few family members that included me. She kept giving attitude while we were there. I remember speaking up for my Uncle because the way they were treating him was wrong as well. Whoever didn't agree with them turned into their enemy. This was my maternal grandmother who I spent the most time with and so I wasn't going to let the bad attitudes of my aunt's get in the way of why I was there!

Everyone chose a part of the house to clean. I picked my old room which was the den at the time. With all the tension going on and people now starting to come visit, I decided my safe haven would be in the den. I didn't want to leave the house so I figured I would stay out the way. Everything was perfect while I was in the den. As I'm just sitting there looking through items, two of my closest friends, Dena, and Stephaine, along with my daughter's grandmother and cousin, Roschell (who is more like an aunt), and my big cousin came in. Roschell Aunt Sue supported me from the time I had my daughter. Aunt Sue passed away and Roschell hasn't skipped a beat.

The den is directly across from the steps so I could see anyone walking up. We hugged and they gave me their condolences. They sat down and we started talking. My uncle came in and sat with us for a while.

My grandmother had six children but when she passed it seemed to me as if she only had two. My aunts took over the second my grandmother closed her eyes! Things were done the way they wanted, not the way my grandmother would have wanted. She would be disgusted to see the division it caused within the family.

While in the room, one of my aunt's walks up and down the steps about four times in a 45 minute period. Just to create a visual for you, she would basically come upstairs and go in the room next to the den where we were. She only stayed a few minutes each time.

She would walk up without looking in the room we were in and when she would come back out she would just walk back down. When she came up the fourth time everything was the same except before going back downstairs, she came into the room this time that we are in and tells everyone that they have to go downstairs.

We looked at her then everyone looked at me. My uncle asked, "Why?"

My aunt responded, "Because I said so."

I said, "We aren't going anywhere."

She stated, "I don't want anything to go missing." Everyone in that room had been in that room prior. We were all together whether it was for parties, holidays, family gatherings, etc., because they all knew my grandmother. Nothing was going to happen, but she was being controlling.

My daughter was witnessing all of this and getting upset. I was more hurt because while they are trying to hurt me they are not caring that they are hurting my daughter, the niece they are supposed to love so much. That was her family that she was mistreating .

My daughter's grandmother, being the eldest in the room, just told everyone to just get up! Everyone gave me a hug, and they all walked down the steps and out the door.

Meanwhile my aunt and I are still going back and forth, and then my other aunt arrives. Of course, they began to team up on me. I asked either of them if they had executive papers. She said yes, but we never did see any!

I remember after finally leaving my grandmother's house going to apologize to my daughter's family for being mistreated when they were only trying to support my family. I felt so bad.

Two of my aunts began to go through my grandmother's things. She made it clear before she passed that there were particular things she wanted people to have. My grandmother always said that she wanted her house to remain a family home for anyone who needed a place to stay. She wanted her house to have peace and love in it. That is the opposite of what we were doing.

My aunts were still going through her items. My grandmother had nicknames for everyone. My daughter's nickname was "Frog." My grandmother had several banks that were in the shape of frogs on her drawer for my daughter's college education.

They didn't give us anything. However, from what I was told everyone else with the exception of my mother and brother received something to remember my grandmother. Without having access to executive papers or something from my grandma saying those were reserved for my daughter, there was nothing I could do to prove they were hers. They were keeping the piggy banks as a means to hurt me. I was heartbroken for my daughter. I have never involved kids in adult problems.

My grandmother passed away a few days after my daughter graduated high school so clearly she was old enough to understand what was going on and she shouldn't have had to mourn her great-grandmother and have money stolen from her that her great-grandmother wanted her to have. It made things more painful for me and my daughter. It was hard to sleep that night. I woke up the next day with a broken heart.

That weekend my daughter graduated high school and my son graduated from preschool. My daughter was having her final recital and my grandmother didn't talk or show much emotion, but she did get to see my daughter in her cap and gown!

About a week later, I was seated on one side of her and one of my aunts was seated on the other side. I was sitting there, holding her hand and I just kept looking at her and her breaths got shorter and shorter and shorter until they just stopped. I let out a huge sigh. I'll always remember that I was there, looking at her in the face while she passed.

Pause For Reflection

Is there anyone that has passed away in your
life that still causes pain or sadness for you?
Write it out. Release it!

_____

_____

_____

_____

_____

_____

_____

_____

_____

_____

_____

_____

_____

_____

Ask God to come into your heart and to fill those voids, and He will. I know it hurts but give it to God. I'm a product of what God can do for matters of the heart.

You may feel your grief will never end, but the Bible promises that joy will eventually come back to you. So with you, now is your time of grief but I will see you again and you will rejoice, and no one will take away your joy. John 16:22

"Ask God to come into your heart and to fill those voids, and He will."

~Towanna Pressley

Chapter 5

After Divorce, Dear God

Life moved on and time went on. I met someone who I thought I was going to spend the rest of my life with.

At this point 95% of the men I dated were into the street so I thought he would have been a little better. The other men I had been with were living very dangerous lives. As I matured, my thought process began to change. I had a human life I was responsible for, so I wanted to make better decisions. I was always told that I had no patience and I needed to compromise a lot more than what I was doing. So let me introduce you to the man I married.

I met him when I was younger, he's my cousin's best friend. We started dating in 2006. I have always been attracted to darker skin men and he was really dark, haha. But more importantly I thought he had to be different. He grew up in a two parent household where his mother and father were together until the day his father passed. His father was a very hard working man who took care of his family. I have never heard anything bad about him.

The house his mother lives in today is the same house he went to straight from the hospital. He is the youngest of four sons so I wasn't surprised to find out that he was spoiled but I didn't think he would still be acting like a big kid in his late 30's early 40's.

He didn't have any children, so he was pretty used to only having himself to worry about. Being raised in a house with a positive male role model, I thought that although he was not my son's biological father he would still possess the fatherly traits. We dated for a few years, and he asked me to marry him.

We were married on October 27, 2011, but only five months later we separated because of the way he treated me. I wouldn't say he treated me bad. I never had the cheating and disrespectful issue that I had with others. I think our priorities were opposite.

Family has and will always be most important to me. He wanted to hang out with his friends and drink. He gave me money for bill, but when it came to anything else we would bump heads. I don't want to spend much time on that. I will just say our priorities didn't align with each other. I remember the Easter Sunday I got upset with him.

I don't remember what I was doing but he told me that he was going to help my cousin move some furniture. This would not have been an issue if he helped around the house that he lived in, and it wasn't a holiday. Both of us were raised that Sunday is family day. I figured out that he is nothing like his father. Easter Sunday, after I said what I said to him regarding leaving, I was ticked off because I remember him leaving anyway. I will always remember the words my ex-husband said to me that day that I knew we were done!

I said something as he was walking up the street. He turned around and said, "I guess you're going to blame this on your childhood too." I felt betrayed. It took me over twenty years to speak my truth. Without hesitation he referenced it in sarcasm. That hurt me badly and I no longer looked at him the same, I knew I could not trust him with my heart.

I was starting to attempt to heal from my childhood and he was one of the first people I told. I was done with him! We separated in April of 2012. The divorce was final June 19, 2013. I haven't looked back to him since.

Pause For Reflection

Write a letter to release the pain.

Dear God,

_____

_____

_____

_____

_____

_____

_____

_____

_____

_____

_____

_____

Dear God,

There are so many things in my life that have hurt me. I am still working on my relationship with one sister, and I had to make peace with the fact that the other one simply doesn't like me. This upsets me because my nieces and nephews suffer. I want everyone to be happy even if their happiness doesn't include me.

The day I caught my ex(we will call him W.K.) on the porch with another female that was half our age. Basically he told me that he loved her. I was mad and heart broken. But sad to say I am used to men disappointing me.

I was hurt the day my daughter's aunt called her on her twenty-seventh birthday with " say, she say." On March 13, 2018, I woke up to a group text from my daughter's cousin who is more like an aunt to my daughter than a cousin. Included in this group text were my daughter, her father, aunt, grandmother, and myself.

Apparently my daughter's aunt was involved in some he say she say and repeated it to the cousin. To a point I don't think my daughter's grandmother and aunt are a fan of the relationship she has with the cousin. So basically the aunt called the cousin with gossip. The gossip hurt the cousin's feelings, so she decided to send a group text expressing how she felt. There was some back and forth in the group between me and the aunt.

The grandmother or father never said a word. My daughter's aunt sent her a disrespectful text separately. My daughter was supposedly talking bad about her cousin and lying on her father. The grandmother and aunt were talking about me and my daughter like dogs, as if they knew the truth.

Apparently my daughter's father was lying saying that he was doing things for her that he really wasn't. I was blamed for things I had no idea of. The argument got really ugly. Although I have always made sure that my daughter knew who her family was, the bond that should be there was not there at all. Instead of accepting the fact that they simply did not play a big role in her life, and that's the reason she doesn't connect with them, they would rather blame me for it.

So when her aunt tried to destroy my daughter's birthday first thing in the morning (before 10 a.m.) with all that negativity it made me angry. It took a little over two years, but the aunt finally apologized, and we are good. I had a discussion with my daughter about what was going on. When she told me that she was upset and didn't know what they were talking about I responded on her behalf. I am so proud of my daughter because she does not allow these types of things to affect her. It may upset her for the moment, but she will speak on it and continue her day!

Then there was the day my stepfather came to visit. He and my sister got into it. My sister decided to go get my mother from her house knowing that would just add more drama. My father had his "then" women with him. They are now yelling and screaming in front of my house. I was pregnant with my son too.

I don't remember what was said right before my sister yelled "Towanna is not even your real daughter!". That was a big shock and a big sting! I just couldn't even believe that was said. Whether true or not, who says that and says it like that? I was so embarrassed.

It hurt the day my aunt put me and my daughter out! I was around twenty-one years old, and my daughter was about a year and a half old. My aunt came home. I went to get my WIC. I had just come back home, and the phone rang. I put my bags down with all the milk and other grocery items in it. I was talking on the phone for a few minutes when my aunt walked in.

My aunt saw the bags on the floor and immediately began yelling at me. She was upset because I hadn't put the milk away and so we started arguing. One thing led to another, and my aunt just said, "you know what, get out!" That really hurt that day because my grandmother was actually with my aunt when all this was happening and I had my baby there, not like it was just me. You didn't at least care about my baby?

I couldn't believe they didn't care. My grandmother and my aunt were getting ready to go out to dinner. My aunt had just told me to get my stuff, so I started packing up everything to leave and did you know they still got themselves ready and went outside to get in the car to leave to go eat like nothing had happened. They saw me walking out with my stuff and my daughter and they just got in the car and left. Didn't even look back!

There was a lady that lived across the street named Mrs. Cassandra Horn. She was in the house at the end of the block, and she didn't have a whole lot, but she was the only one who saw me and cared enough to have us come and stay with them because she didn't want us on the street.

She offered the little bit that she had to help. We didn't stay there long. My daughter and I stayed there for about a week. To this day I'm still close to her family. Mrs. Horn's oldest daughter became like my sister. Mrs. Horn actually passed away a couple years ago, but it meant a lot to me that she let us stay.

After we left there , we went and stayed at my friend/cousin Chris' house for a couple weeks. Then we ended up on my grandmother's block at my girlfriend's house. We were there for maybe two weeks.

After a while, the block starts talking. I got a message from my grandmother saying that we can come and stay there until we find somewhere to go. Now we had been roaming around, at this point sleeping from house to house for over a month! You went to dinner with my aunt and didn't care about us and now all of a sudden that people in the neighborhood are starting to talk and you know it's making you look bad, now you extend the invitation?

I felt that was the only reason. I decided to call my daughter's father's mother and asked her if we could stay there, and she actually told me "no." That was another thing that hurt. I could see if she told me I couldn't come, but she didn't care that her granddaughter was homeless with me and had nowhere to go. That really hurt. Yet she went on to continue caring for all her other grandchildren that she had. It is what it is now but when it happened it hurt.

My paternal grandmother (the mother of the man on my birth certificate) got wind of this and told me to start looking for my first apartment for me and my daughter. Going to wash my clothes around the street is how I ran into Tiana!

We stayed there for about 3 years and then we moved a couple blocks away and we stayed in the next place for about 4 years. When we left we moved with my maternal grandmother because I wanted to buy a house. We stayed around two years. I worked two jobs and I saved up enough money to buy my own house. On April 30th, 1999 ,I closed on my first home! That was my little bit of joy in the middle of all the storms. It hurt being a single mom while two men were fully capable of taking care of their children.

I planned a surprise party for my ex when we were still together. He showed no appreciation then a few days later he got into an argument with one of the six mothers of his children, and she decided to call me to tell me what he was up to.

She told me that he knew about the party and didn't want to attend. He even told her the only reason he attended was because his money probably paid for it anyway. I was very offended because I invested a lot of time and money to make it special. And I did not use his money for any of it.

It hurts that I didn't have a constant father figure because my mother took me from the only stable place I had known. I feel like I'm finally healing from that. It hurts that my mother was not there for my first heartbreak. It also hurts that she wasn't there when I was in labor with my first child!

It hurts when I think about my ex. We will call this Ex "Lesson". I remember myself and Lesson going on a cruise. While on the cruise, I found out that he went to his child's house at 8 in the morning. I knew nothing about it.

He and the child's mother were texting telling each other they loved each other while he was on the trip with me, and I found the messages. He felt as if it was meaningless. After explaining to him that this was the same child's mother that had been disrespecting me so there was a big issue. He still didn't care! My advice to anyone in a relationship, although you will not agree with everything, do not allow yourself to stay with someone that does not make protecting your heart and feelings a number one priority!

Several women in Lesson's life have caused me hurt and pain. They would call and tell me that he was at their homes and bringing them money. They would also call and tell me that they were having sex with him. Some would even tell me what I cooked for dinner. He never admitted anything. Everyone was lying on him and full of crap but really he was the one that was. I invested a lot in that relationship. He figured since he helped pay bills (I mean only helped; he never paid all my bills) and cooked really well that was enough to erase all the disrespect. But this relationship taught me the most.

It hurt that one year around Christmas time, my mother bought the entire family Christmas presents a few years back and left my children out because she was mad at me! She took it out on my innocent children.

There was another time that hurt pertaining to Tiana. My daughter needed somewhere to park her car because she was having registration issues. My mother had private parking in the back of her house. My daughter asked if she could park her car there. My mother said yes at first.

A week or so later, my mother got upset with my daughter and threatened to have her car towed if she didn't move it. I think that's something awful to do to your granddaughter! My daughter drove my car and I drove her to a new location. We drove at night. She followed close behind me until we reached the destination. I thanked God for protecting us from being stopped by the police or getting in an accident. That would have been bad with no tags on the car.

It hurt having abortions….it really hurt.

It hurt going down Broad and Erie Avenue knocking on crack house doors looking for my mother and she would tell people to tell me that she wasn't there. What kind of mother just abandons her child and then when her child needs her tells people to tell me that she's gone. This used to break my heart. I would still keep looking for her.

It makes me angry that when I was older and lived on my own , I would let my mother come visit during her addiction and she would steal my things. I remember one time I let her come and stay. I had a nice leather trench coat hanging up. I had to go to the bathroom. When I came out my mother had on my coat and went running past me saying "I'll be right back." She never came back and never brought my coat and some of my other things back. This really disappointed me that she would steal from me when I was trying to be there for her.

It hurts that I was molested and raped. I blocked out the different molestations but not the rape. It wasn't until I actually spoke the words out loud around 2007, that I was able to allow myself to feel anything. Once I began to feel I became full of guilt. I believe that a molester will continue to molest until they are caught. I felt like I could have saved some other people's lives because my heart tells me that he did not stop with me. I should have said something.

It hurts when I think about my kids. I feel like I failed my kids, especially my son. I've apologized to them so many times for not choosing better fathers. All the yelling and screaming. The work I have been doing the past 4 years is not only for me but for them as well. I hope they are able to forgive me for any mistakes I made with raising them.

I was very angry the day my daughter's father put the mother of his wife before his daughters. My daughter and her sister were having a fundraiser to help her brother out. My daughter's father owned the building. But no one stepped up to help her but me.

We got to the building, and they were going to be serving food. Chips, hotdogs, hoagies, etc. The mother in law saw me and apparently didn't like me. I didn't even realize who she was. My daughter and her sister spoke to her. I saw the lady and I spoke to her, but she didn't speak back to me, but I thought it was just me.

The mother n law used the building often and would make dinners and sold them out of the building. So my daughter and her sister asked the mother n law for a pot to boil the hotdogs. She gets an attitude and says we cannot cook there. Now mind you this is their step grandmother. Tiana was wiping ketchup off the floor, and she approached her asking her if something was wrong in an arrogant tone. Hearing how she addressed my child I approached her and just simply asked her if she could please give them a pot!

So one thing led to another, and she called the father. She lies and says that we're down there starting trouble and that wasn't true we literally just wanted to boil hot dogs lol. So when her father comes , he tells my daughter "If you have it here your mom can't stay". My daughter told me she let him know that due to me being her only help for an event that was to raise money for his son that she would have it elsewhere. The entire incident was confusing because I honestly didn't know who she was when we first arrived. I simply said hello. I didn't pay attention to if she spoke back but as time went on of course I realized who she was and realized she didn't speak back. Because of her attitude I realized that I was the problem.

I have supported my daughter with everything she has done big or small since birth and I won't stop until I can't. Little do they know if anyone would have volunteered to help them that day I would have been more than happy to sit at home. That was my plan for that day!

No one was there to help. NO ONE except guess who? Her cousin Roschell who made a salad. Roschell is always there for us. Over the years we grew so close that you would really think we shared the same DNA. We used to fight and make up all the time.

When Tiana was little Roschell used to be at our apartment all the time. We used to get in some good trouble. But this day for some reason she forgot who I was as a person and decided to believe what she heard. We never got the salad, and she would not answer any of my phone calls. Apparently Tiana's grandmother had called her with a false story of what happened, and Roschell believed them.

Other than that it was just her and her sister. So yes as a mother I did what I was supposed to do.

I'm trying to reason with him and I'm asking him are you serious? It's your building and your daughter and they are down here trying to help their brother. So I called my aunt and asked her if my daughter and her sister could come there to boil the hotdogs since the pot seemed to be an issue.

So at this point I'm pleading with him not to kick them out, but he still ends up saying no and doesn't let them use the building anymore. Meanwhile my daughter was mad and outside hurt. They had already put out flyers and everything. She had already spent her own money to pay for things and she only had a part time job at McDonald's, and he still didn't care.

So I decided to let her move everything to my house. But meanwhile the address on the flier was for her father's building. So we hurry up and get to my house and print off a new flier with my home address and put it on the door of her father's building so everyone would know where to go.

Then we came back to my house. My daughter forgot something at her father's building, and when she got there she saw the flyers had been taken down. To me that was just evil, and I was pissed.

My daughter didn't make much money, and she ended up losing money and not making money. Later on down the line I started hearing that the grandmother and the aunt were saying that I took all the money which was not true! There was a $5 charge for people to get in. I didn't keep anything. I even paid my daughter to come into my own house! That's how much I supported her.

Within the last few years I was hurt and angry to find out that for thirty years my daughter's grandmother spread lies about me. She thought I reported her for fraud but that is not my character. Maybe she felt that way out of guilt for not being there when me and her granddaughter needed her when we had nowhere to go. She pretty much has had a love hate relationship for me ever since. All for something I never did.

I release the pain.

I release the hurt.

I release the shame.

I release it all and I forgive who I need to forgive. I give it to God, and I let Him have it. He's bigger than any problem or situation.

I am not my past.

I am more than enough, and I am better than who I was yesterday.

I'm growing and changing daily, and I know God is going to do even more through me.

Signed,
Towanna

Pause For Reflection

Take the next couple of pages to write out your own Dear God letter of the things that hurt you and who you need to forgive and then let it go!

_____

_____

_____

_____

_____

_____

_____

_____

_____

_____

_____

_____

_____

_____

Chapter 6

Parenting Relationships After Trauma

There were a lot of ways that all of the trauma affected me as a child. It completely wiped out my memory because I don't remember half of it. It created trust issues. It didn't allow me to be a kid! I really don't even know what it feels like to just be a kid.

Growing up when I started liking boys I had to create my own vision as to what that should look like. I didn't have a blueprint as to how it should go because I had no real male role models.

As I got older and started talking to boys/young men I realized quickly that it wasn't the perfect picture I envisioned. I was hurt so many times and now that I'm older I realized I settled a lot as well simply just wanted to be loved. Because I felt abandoned and useless at times I would attach myself to anyone that showed attention to me. I would mistake that for love. I would invest all my extra time and energy on that relationship that 90% of the time ended up with me being hurt.

Being molested mentally damaged my brain in certain areas mainly sex and trust. I try so hard to trust people, but I constantly find myself always with one eye open and once I catch you in a lie I will never fully trust you again. Then there is sex. I have had sex yes, but I can go months even years without it. I love hard so when in a relationship I will make it enjoyable for my mate other than that I really didn't care.

I've been dumb and stupid for love at times falling for the lines "I don't love her", "I'm only there for the kids, "I'm leaving etc. All the lies men tell to keep you from leaving them. Then there's the disrespect you tolerate because you think you're in love.

You stay in that relationship hoping for change that will never come. I'm proud to say that TODAY I am no longer interested in any man that has any type of abnormal relationships with anyone of any kind.

I know as an adult , I still have trust issues. I didn't learn how to love myself until just recently. I'm sure I'm not the only one.

I know I have always been a people pleaser because of it. I have always cared about whether everybody else was okay and happy before worrying about my own happiness. I didn't care about me. If I could do it for somebody else I would, even if it meant burning myself out. It has greatly played a part in me being controlling. I believe in "don't wait." Get it done if you can fix it now then do it. That goes for everything and everybody. This makes relationships difficult for me with family, friends, and men because everybody does not think that way or see things that way.

For most of my life I haven't had any self-worth. I grew up for a long time living with low self-esteem and no self-love. I always felt like that if my parents didn't love me then why should anybody else love me? Why should I love myself?

I have had men in my life who probably really did care about me, but I wasn't able to accept it as love because I didn't really know how to receive real love. And on the other hand I haven't had one where I didn't end up getting hurt, cheated on or lied to. This in turn has made me bitter and mean at times.

I have always thought that I explain things and give a lot of details. I'm direct and straight to the point. Sometimes it gets on people's nerves but whenever I haven't been detailed people get upset with me or say that "I didn't communicate or give them more information." So now I'm overly detailed. But that doesn't matter either because I'm realizing people are not listening. I hate repeating myself.

I have also noticed that I internalize things a lot and I try to deal with a lot of stuff on my own. And I tend to let things build up on the inside. Especially when it comes to really, really serious situations. I have a hard time expressing myself and when it finally comes out, it comes out as anger.

I often feel that people simply DO NOT care about how they make others feel. Whether on purpose or not you still should acknowledge a situation. People get mad at my responses to certain things but don't acknowledge what they did to upset me or make me say something in the first place. At least that's how my brain interprets it. I don't feel they have the right to tell me how I need to deliver it if they are the ones that have caused the hurt.

I used to hold things in a lot until I realized that it was starting to affect my health. It was causing me to feel sick and it was giving me migraines. I speak out but I hold stuff in just as much. The stress was too much.

I know that I was depressed. And to be honest I feel like I may have been depressed my entire life. I know that when I was really depressed I could lay in the bed and not eat or drink and just lay in the bed for twenty-four hours straight. Sometimes just drink a Pepsi and be done for the day and not want anything else. Literally I could go from 160 pounds to 115 pounds in what seemed like over a few days or a weekend.

People have always called me angry or mean or nasty. I hear that a lot. But most people haven't had to go through the level of trauma that I have or if they have they just have responded differently. Everyone responds to trauma differently. I guess for me, it made me "mean." I remember when I had my daughter my cousin William went and told my family that after I had my daughter that " I didn't have an attitude anymore" everyone thought that was so funny.

I was always in bad relationships though. I wanted the thugs and the street guys. The ones that were able to buy me stuff and hold me down and take care of me, but they also cheated on me all the time. But those are the guys I would date. They were toxic for me but unfortunately I craved the street men.

I know it's because of the level of dysfunction that I had in my childhood. My view of affection was distorted. My view of love was tainted, and my innocence was demolished. So I honestly didn't know what I was doing when it came to the opposite sex.

I would always be called insecure in my relationships. They would always tell me that I need patience and to compromise. I didn't want to give up on relationships so I would continue to try but only to be hurt again. I endured pain and vulgarity.

I can say one of the pluses is that after my last relationship, I have been celibate, and I haven't been with anyone in three years. No dating or anything. I have dealt with so much toxicity I decided to take some time and work on myself so that when I do get into another relationship, I will actually love myself this time and not put up with a bunch of stuff.

This time, I have decided that I will give it all to God and that I'm not looking for anybody. I told God that I want him to send him. And he will have to confirm to me that he's the one whenever he does show up. If I don't get that sense of discernment, and that feeling in my heart and in my gut then I don't want to be bothered! So for now I'm waiting.

I didn't know there was such a thing as betrayal trauma and I'm learning about that now. I now know that is something that I struggle with and of course the root of betrayal trauma is rejection and betrayal. Definitely something I have worked on the last few years in releasing from my life.

The emotional and mental abuse is something else! I have endured over and over again and that has played a part in how I process things. I have become very moody because of it. And I have become very irritable. But I can honestly say that I have healed tremendously. I'm not perfect and I still have my moments. But I'm much happier now.

Parenting After Trauma

Dealing with all the trauma I dealt with as a child, I feel like it helped to make me strong as a parent, but I know that I wasn't the perfect parent. I struggled a lot.

I remember that I got pregnant with my daughter, and I was so scared and nervous. I was so terrified of my family finding out, but I was mortified at the thought of my grandmother hearing the news. I knew she would be mad, and I didn't know how she would react. I also didn't feel like I was ready for a baby. I knew she would be highly upset with me.

Sure enough her response to me blew me away! My mother always told me that when she was pregnant with me that my grandmother put her out. My grandmother denied it and said that my mother was lying. I was not prepared for her to do that to me.

My mom said my grandmother told her that she was not bringing a bastard child into her house. My grandmother always denied that as well. But I still always carried this in the back of my mind!

That day in March of 1991, about a week before my delivery date, my grandmother said those same words to me. I remember this clear as day. My grandmother's house had two sets of steps. I was coming down the back steps which lead to the kitchen. About four steps from the bottom my grandmother looked at me and said, "Well do you know where you're going" I responded by asking her what she meant by that then she said, "you're not bringing a bastard child in my house!" I remember that it hurt so bad!

I was well into my thirties when I finally brought up that conversation and how it made me feel. I was surprised and hurt when my grandmother told me that she never told me that either.

These words hurt me to my core. They shook me in places I didn't know that I could be shook. The time came for me to give birth to my daughter. I remember what I was doing the day I went into labor and had my daughter. My daughter was born March 13, 1991, at 12:41 in Lankenau Hospital. Since my grandmother had put me out about a week earlier, I stayed with my aunt, and she was out of town on business the week of my due date. I didn't want to be alone in case I went into labor, so stayed at my friend D'Nae's house.

Mike Tyson was on TV fighting. I remember that I was on her daybed, she had one of those beds that had the metal poles/bars attached to it, and I was laying on her bed and I felt my first contractions! The pain hit me, and I yelled out! It was so bad, that I ended up grabbing the bars on her bed and breaking them because of how bad it hurt. So we ended up heading to the hospital. I was admitted that night.

Dnae left because the policy was only one person in the room with me and that was my daughter's father. Her father had two other kids by someone else before I got pregnant, but he wasn't able to be there for their births. So it was kind of special because she was his first daughter and the first one that he actually was able to see being born.

He was so nervous that day. The nurses had asked him to help me by giving me the ice chips in my mouth in between pushing and it was funny because he was so nervous and trying to watch me push Tiana out that he was getting ice chips all over my face and totally missing my mouth! Lol. Then as he saw her crown and started to come out he started yelling eeew, eeewww. Then he said "I ain't never going in there again!"

Everyone froze and looked at me to see my reaction as if they may have thought I was going to be upset but I just burst out laughing and then he laughed and everyone else laughed and I went ahead and pushed her completely out.

He left the hospital a little while after she was born to go get cigars. He came back to the hospital that night and said he wanted to stay there with us overnight. But instead of him telling them he was the father , he ended up telling them he was my brother or something, so they ended up not letting him stay all because he lied! He thought being my brother was more important than the child's father. He was back first thing the next morning and we laughed about it.

When he got there I left him with Tiana and went into the bathroom to freshen up. As I was coming out of the bathroom the assistant was preparing to take Tiana back to the nursery. As she was being rolled out I noticed that her name card had been filled out, so I asked that she be rolled back to me. I picked the card to see where this man filled the card out. His name is Steven and for some reason he thought I was having a boy whose name was going to be Stefon. He was going to name the boy and I was going to name the girl. So when the baby came out he tried to renege. This man named my child Stefano Tiana Westbrook.

I'm so glad I caught that, if not I would have killed him (lolol). Our compromise ended up being Tiana Monique Stefona Westbrook. We both won. The day came that we were being discharged. I remember bundling Tiana up well because it was cold and raining. My aunt Liza (my uncle's spouse for years) was there to pick us up. This would be Tiana's finder, the bender. Although my grandmother had put me out her house was still the first place I went. When we got on the block my aunt attempted to make a U-turn and crashed into a car in the process. I laughed about that for years.

Tiana's father and I met back in 1989, two years after I met Maurice (Tyreece's dad). Ty Reece's father ended up back in jail. One night Lisa and I went out to two popular bars, Dixon's, and Club Hawks. This is where I met him. I remember Lisa used to get her step-father's car, we would put the top down and ride back and forth between our house and the neighborhood he lived in. We did this all day long. It was so much fun. Those were the good old days.

In 1990 it was time for my prom. I asked him to go, and he said yes, but at this time he was heavy in the streets so a part of me thought he was going to stand me up, so I asked someone else who also said yes.

The day of prom came and although I talked to him, and he confirmed he would be there I still wasn't convinced. After 7:00 that night he called to tell me he was on his way. Ten minutes later the other guy called to tell me that he was across the street at the payphone. I remember lying even pretending to be crying telling him that my dress was messed up and that I was not going. I felt so bad but the person I really wanted to go was on his way.

Around 7:45 I got downstairs to take pictures and leave. I was so happy, smiling from ear to ear. Finally we get outside in the car and leave. I really had fun. Lisa and a few other friends met us at the prom to take more pictures knowing they weren't supposed to be there. The next day the other guy called to let me know that he never left and that he watched me leave. I didn't know what to say. I've seen him a couple times over the years and every single time I apologize more.

After my daughter was born a lot changed inside of me. I always felt that I was fighting emotionally. My body was getting older, but my heart still needed so much healing. I was broken inside. I had nowhere to turn. I ended up getting pregnant by her father again, sadly I made the decision to get an abortion. And I continued on the path of pain and internal destruction and mental warfare.

My life was literally a blur during that time! I was in so much darkness and depression. Before I knew it, I was pregnant again. I still can't believe it! Clearly it was an indicator of my self-esteem.

I had three abortions and two miscarriages putting my life in danger and no one to run to. No one! There was no one to hold me and say it would be okay. No one told me I was worth more than what I was doing and allowing a man to do whatever they wanted to me. There was no one to tell me what my value was. I had no one to sing love over me and embrace me and show me what real love was supposed to feel like. I was lost.

I had no idea what real love was supposed to feel like. I created my own versions of love. Tiana was my world. Nothing or no one came before her. She became my reason to fight.

Pause For Reflection

Have you ever found yourself in a place where you felt confused, lost, and broken? Where were you? What happened?

Use this next section to write about the times in your life when you have felt broken and lost. Writing and confessing is an important part of your breakthrough. After you write it, release it to God and ask God to heal the wounds.

_____

_____

_____

_____

_____

_____

_____

_____

_____

_____

_____

Every day was a journey and a learning experience, and they had to be a part of my errors and my flaws as I tried every day to just figure out life. I was the best parent considering what I went through.

My children often tell me that I was tough on them. I was! I didn't make any mess. I would be quick to get upset or fuss at them about something, no matter how small of an issue it was. It was tough. I wasn't one to be played with.

I was also very loving as well and nurtured them as much as I could and did my best to give them what I didn't have growing up. I did my best to give them stability when it was within my power to do so.

There were so many good memories with my kids though even in the midst of it. I remember giving my daughter a special party with Barney and she was so happy and thrilled but yelled as loud as she could when Barney came near her. Another party I made sure the power rangers were there and she was thrilled about that! I think she was the Pink Ranger.

I remember when I took my kids to open up their own savings accounts. I did my best to always be present. Whether it was dance recitals, or sports teams or dance or anything I was always there for my kids. I never missed a beat when they were involved in anything.

I always wanted my son and my daughter and their friends to feel safe when they came over to my house. I would talk to the other parents to make sure they felt comfortable leaving their kids at my house.

I'll never forget when my daughter Tiana was about eleven-years-old, and she was at drill practice outside and she got hit by a car! I was at the grocery store when I got the call that she was being rushed to the hospital. I dropped my groceries and ran out the store. I got to that hospital as quickly as I could. I was worried about her. Thank God she ended up being okay. After that I told off her drill team sergeant that she will never tag outside again! I made sure of that.

I took parenting seriously, and I didn't play about my kids sneaking at all behind my back. I was going through my daughter's phone, and I figured out that she had snuck a boy in her room, so I took her Jr Prom away from her! She was mad and crying real bad. I was also upset and hurt too because I was looking forward to her prom. I know she can't get that prom back, but I was so serious about that kind of stuff. I still feel that the consequences matched the offense. I was looking forward to her prom and I do feel robbed of that opportunity to share that moment with her.

I made sure I was present for events for my kids when I was able to be there. I always gave them my presence if nothing else.

One day I got upset and called my daughter a B. And to this day she still remembers, and she held onto that for a while. I feel bad for doing that. I wish I could take it back. I made up for a lot of it for her senior prom. I went out of the way, to give her the prom that she wanted. I made sure she had the dress, the car, the shoes , everything she wanted and needed. I was a proud mother and I always wanted them to know I was proud. I did my best to comfort them whenever they went through things.

I remember one day my daughter found out that her friend got killed and I was there for her every step of the way. I helped her get through it. I love my kids and would do anything for them.

One of the special memories was that when my daughter was in college she was a part of

Ziana (The Fashion Club). She was in it for all 4 years. They would have midnight fashion shows which never started on time, but I made all four of them. I would drive an hour and half there and be there for the show and then drive all the way back and then have to be at work at 8:00 in the morning! I think I was one of the only parents that would actually come for the shows.

According to my son, growing up in the same household with me definitely isn't easy. I can be bossy and controlling and it drives them crazy. But that's just who I am. I do believe in working on myself, and I have been doing that the last few years!

Raising my children, I made sure that they always knew I wanted what was best for them and now they are both that way. We all want what's best for each other.

My son had to grow up without his dad, but we were always together when he was younger so there's so many memories and connections with him.

I pushed him to be active and a participant in the social world. Almost every year I had him in a new activity. Seriously! I wanted him to be well rounded. He has played soccer, lacrosse, baseball, boxing, taken piano lessons and he will tell you that I never let him give up.

He was always mad because I made him do things that he didn't want to do, but it was only because I wanted him to thrive. No matter what age he was, I made sure he was always involved in something so he wouldn't be lazy.

Listen, I went to every field trip he's ever had since preschool. I didn't care if he wanted me to be present or not, I wanted him to know that mama was going to be there. He appreciates this now that he's older.

I was at every parent-teacher conference, and I knew all of their teachers! I wanted to make sure they were being the best version of themselves that they could be. I remember when my son started his first candy business I told him that he could stop whenever he wanted. My son claims that no matter how many times he told me he was ready to stop, I would not let him! He was upset that he was forced to do it and he became upset with me. It caused a lot of tension and our relationship started to get rocky but at the end of the day, I was still there for my son. He had a mentor named Nehemiah Davis. He even won the Steve Harvey award.

I can say that when it comes to my children no matter how much we may argue or disagree, I love them, and they love me, and we will always be by each other's side.

Chapter 7

Finding My Biological Father

I was told sometime during my early teens that the man listed on my birth certificate was not my biological father and that my father's name was John Carter. I didn't know whether to believe it or not, so I erased it from my mind.

I remember my paternal grandmother telling me that I looked like several family members who all lived down South. Furney Sutton is the name listed on my birth certificate. When I was around five, my little brother (Furney's son) was born. I was curious why my features didn't look like him, but again I erased it from my mind. At this age I did realize that not all family members looked the same. Somewhere between twelve and sixteen I was staying with my grandmother, Furney's mother.

At this time Furney had his own apartment that he shared with his then girlfriend Stephanie. My grandmother was trying to make him be a responsible father and take me with him. I don't remember if it was to live permanently or for a few days. All I know is that I hated it there and after that second night I hated him. Stephanie and he got into an argument, and she left.

I don't remember what happened before or after, but after she left, he laid me down on his bed and raped me. I remember having resentment towards my grandmother because I felt that if she didn't send me that it would have never happened. I loved her but not too long after he did that to me he moved back into her house. That's when my visits got shorter.

No matter when anyone would visit my grandmother's house they would find Furney sitting in the reclining chair five or maybe six feet from the door. Visiting became somewhat painful. I didn't want to speak to him but felt as if I had no choice. He pretended as if nothing happened and so did I.

I stopped calling him dad and referred to him as Furney. Something else that I felt angry about is that people heard me either acknowledging him as Furney or not at all, but nobody took the time to find out why. What little girl doesn't love her father. Why didn't anybody ask me why I was hostile with him and distant?

I'm not sure of the year mainly because of what he did to me, but I asked my mother if he was my father. At first she denied him not being my father. I let it go. Then in November 1991 my little sister (Furney's daughter) was born. Once again a baby born looking even more like Furney than my brother. I visited the topic with my mother once again, this time I wanted the truth.

I received what I thought was the truth. My mother finally admitted that she was in a bad place in life and really didn't know.

The topic was and still is hard for her to talk about, but she was able to tell me that my grandmother and Furney both knew from the day I was born that I was not biologically theirs. I was told that my grandmother did not care, she just wanted me. This made me love her so much more. During a conversation with my mom discussing the topic I could tell she wanted to say something but couldn't get the courage to say. We made it a judge free zone and she was finally ready to say for the first time. As she cried she told me that she buried things so deep because it hurt so bad. She told me that she was always afraid that I might be GUESS whose child, yup her stepfather. The thought of it made her sick. This was the first time she ever said it out loud.

The story I was told by my aunts and uncle was that my biological fathers name was John Carter and that he served in some form of the military. I was also told that John Carter stopped by my grandmother's house one day to ask my mother if the baby she was carrying was his, and she told him no. And this John person was never seen again. I took this information and searched for John Carter.

My search included locating any military information that was open to the public, finding and looking through old phone books, even knocking on doors in the area where my mother told me he lived.

I met several nice people but none of them were able to help me. I even remember one elder woman who welcomed me into her home. I explained to her the reason for the visit. She began to pull out photo albums and everything. She was excited to think I could be her granddaughter.

I think I forgot to mention that her name was Mrs. Carter. She was the only person I was able to find that had a son named John Carter that did serve in the military. She even gave me a picture of him that I still have to this day. With John Carter being a common name the job was pretty much impossible. I've been told by several people, but I am not completely convinced that John Carter even exists.

My next move was to reach out to the person my mother was best friends with during the time I was conceived. I stopped by her house one day to ask if maybe she knew. At that point she told me that she wasn't sure, however she knew I didn't belong to Furney, and she had never heard of a guy back then named John Carter.

After about 30-40 minutes I gave her my number and asked her if she thought of anything else to please give me a call and I left. When I got into my car she called me.

She began to tell me that when I was walking away I reminded her of a man named Barry. She went on to tell me how I walked like him and that we shared the same hair color. Whoever this Barry guy used to hang out with them back in the day. She really didn't want to get involved so she asked me not to say anything about the visit.

I appreciated her help and understood why she made that request, so I honored it. She said somehow Furney was supposed to have found out that my mother was seeing Barry. Furney supposedly approached this guy and scared him so badly that the man disappeared. I finally thought I was getting somewhere! I called a few times just to ask if she had thought of anything else that could help. She would never answer. I later found out that my sister went behind my back and told my mom. I never found out if that was the reason she stopped answering or not, but I didn't appreciate my sister doing that. That also turned out to be a dead end.

At this point I'm grown and although I wanted to know the truth I began thinking maybe it wasn't meant for me to know. I have family members that felt as if I shouldn't care and couldn't understand why I wanted to know. I thought their opinions were very selfish and inconsiderate. Time was passing. I was getting older which means that this man named Barry was getting older as well. I began to let it go and accept the fact that maybe I would never find out.

Years passed and life went on. I've always been nosy so when the at home DNA kits came onto the market, I wanted to take one just to see what information it could truly give.

Honestly, I never rushed because I didn't believe this take at home test could provide but so much. So I think it was my birthday or Mother's Day some years back when my now ex-boyfriend surprised me with the kit. I was so happy and nervous at the same time. I let the kit sit on my living room table for about a week. One day I looked at the box on the table and told myself, "Stop being scared. Just do it."

I opened the box, read the directions. You had to fill this tube with saliva, place the tube in the shipping package and place it in the mailbox. The instructions said that you would receive your results via email in about two weeks. I was shocked to receive an email in eight days saying that my results were in. I remember telling myself that I knew this was a scheme, because it seemed like I had just mailed it so there's no way (if this was real) that I could receive the results so fast.

Later that night, I sat down and decided to check the email to see what it showed. I was shocked to see so much information. One of the sections was titled "closest relatives." I clicked on it and when I did my heart dropped.

The first person listed said half-sister. I clicked on the button and there was a light skinned female with dirty brown hair. Because I have dirty brown hair and could never figure out where it came from it made my heart drop.

I was still not convinced, but I began looking through the thousand plus people they had listed as relatives. There were several ways to search. One way was the people that shared the most amount of DNA. I clicked that button. Again the female with the half-sister was first. Then there was another female who I identified as my aunt(my mother and her share the same father) then there was a cousin, this cousin is my maternal grandmother's sister's granddaughter . My heart dropped again.

I let a few days go by trying to figure out what to do. During that week I went on Facebook to search for the half-sister's name listed. And there she was again with that same dirty brown hair. After about a week I logged back on the 23 & Me website and sent a message to the female listed as my half-sister.

A few more days passed, and I received an email message from 23 & Me stating that the person had responded to my message. My heart dropped yet again. I know I replied back wanting to have a conversation, I don't remember if she called me, or I called her, but I remember how nervous I was on the phone.

Of course she was confused because no one had ever heard anything about me. As we talked I told her a little about me and what I was looking for. After about 30 mins I finally got the courage to ask that question I had wanted to know the answer to for so long. There was a small pause on the phone and that's when I asked Tanisha what is your father's name?

Tanisha is the name of the person listed as my half-sister. She replied "James Thompson". I repeated "James Thompson" she said "yes." She said James had five other children.

She said he had two sons and three other daughters which is six children total. The names that she knew were Anthony, Nathan, Emma, Tinesha, Tiffany, and Tiana. I didn't know how to feel! I went to bed one night with two brothers and two sisters and woke up with four brothers and six sisters. This information was overwhelming, but I told myself that I asked for the truth!

During our conversation she mentioned where she lived and amazingly I was going to the Casino that night which was literally 5 minutes from her home. So close that you could walk. I remember asking myself if this is really happening. Before we hung up the phone, I asked her if I could stop by on my way passing through and without hesitating she said " yes."

During the ride my heart was racing the entire time. I finally arrived at her house. It had only been minutes, but it felt like hours. I called to tell her I was outside, moments later she and her husband were walking towards me. As she approached we were both looking at each other in amazement.

We went inside and talked for hours. She gave me a little background on what she could. Some of the things were heartbreaking. She told me that she doesn't remember much, herself because she was young. What she could tell me was that James had passed away over twenty years ago from lung cancer and that he was an alcoholic.

She said, "James has a sister that I remember is very nice." She, Tiana, and

Tiffany shared the same mother. Tiffany had recently gotten married and had a baby. I've never met her. Tiana was murdered by her boyfriend a couple years ago. This touched a nerve because my first born child's name is = spelled the same way. No one knows much about Emma besides the fact that she lives in Ohio. She knew nothing about Anthony and the craziest part of this is that Nathan lives within walking distance from my house!

I got on Facebook and sent messages to Tiffany, Emma and Nathan leaving my phone number and explaining the situation. To this day Tiffany hasn't responded. Nathan, on the other hand thought I was a little crazy. He said he showed the message to his wife in disbelief. Shortly after my phone rang and it was Nathan. We didn't stay on the phone long. He asked questions and told me he wanted to come see me. He got here so fast I thought he must have already been outside. We talked so much. He called our cousins who were the daughter and son of the aunt that Taneisha was telling me about. He explained what was going on. Later on my daughter, Nathan and myself decided to go visit the aunt. Her children knew about me, but their mother didn't. They wanted to keep it as a surprise. It took us about thirty minutes to get to her house. As we got closer to the house I realized that she lived literally two blocks from where my aunt (my mother's sister) lived for years. And when I say years I mean at least twenty or more. I would visit my aunt's house very often. So to find out that James lived 5 mins or less walking distance to where I spent a lot of time was another surprise. Not only James but Taneisha, Tiffany and Tiana.

Later I found out that my cousins (my mother's sisters, children) actually knew some of them. I was blown away again. We walked into the house. I stood on the living room floor, and they called for their mom.

A few minutes later a small, framed woman comes down the steps. I said hello, and she said hello back. Everyone besides her starts laughing, then her daughter starts to explain who I am. The family was very welcoming. We all sat down, and I began to share my story.

She pulled out photo albums as well as obituaries. The pictures she had weren't the best, some were ripped, some faded. I don't think I can remember all the people she pointed out to me, but I do remember some. She showed me pictures of her grandmother, her mother, James, and some others I can't remember. I saw James and Tiana's obituaries. Tiana's was still like new, but James' was torn. It was so bad that I couldn't really make out what he looked like. Besides the obituary there was one other picture, but the quality was bad. They gave me a little history about James.

James was a long distance truck driver. In the early 70's he lived in a house on Catharine St. between 62nd & 63rd St. He was married to Anthony's mother, and they shared that house until they broke up. When they broke up he moved in with his grandmother Emma Thompson at 6034 Master St. They told me that the house we were standing in actually belonged to their mother Kate Thompson who left it to James. I was blown away!

James got married again and gave the house to his sister and moved around the corner. They told me he died from I believe some form of cancer due to drinking. We stayed there for two hours, talking.

The discussion turned on James and my mother. When I was looking at James' obituary his date of birth was unreadable. I told them that my mother got pregnant at the age of 15 and gave birth at 16. As I said that out loud I remembered hearing that James was in his 80's when he died. That meant when my mother was 15, James was in his thirties.

After being molested by Furney, I had days; that I wished he was not my father! After finding out that both my grandmother and Furney knew from the start that I was not biologically his daughter, I convinced myself that maybe that's why he felt as if it was okay to violate me in such a tragic way. He knew I was not his. So finding out the truth was important to me. I didn't want to go my entire life thinking that the man that was supposed to protect me was the one I needed to be protected from!

That honestly became the number one reason for me wanting to know. Now I know the truth! Something about James and my mother's age difference did not sit well with me. However ,knowing that my mother was put out of the house at twelve, I guess she had to find ways to survive. She was molested by her stepfather.

While visiting my aunt I used my phone to take pictures of her. I later showed my mother a picture of James, she still had no clue who he was! Sometimes I wonder if she also blocked her experiences out because of the impact the trauma had on her. Who knows!

I remember searching for my " real " father but not going that hard because my grandmother was alive and if this information were true I did not in any way want to hurt her. So once she passed I put a little more pressure on myself . Not realizing that she knew from the beginning.

I was later told that she knew from the day I was born that I was not biologically hers, but she wanted me anyway! I believe that had I told her what was going on that she would have done something about it!

Some of my initial thoughts the second I found out were what would my other siblings think, how would they feel? I was a little more concerned with my siblings that were Furney's biological kids. I wasn't sure how they would take the news. I actually considered burying the truth, finding peace within myself, and not telling anyone. I did not want anyone to hurt like I was. As long as I knew that would be all that mattered. It did give me peace to finally know the truth but not the type of peace that I was expecting! It hurts to find out the truth.

Not knowing who my real father was all those years really put me in a state of false identity and rejection. Most little girls yearn to have a daddy daughter relationship and I didn't get to have that.

Not having your father can leave voids that are unimaginable. But the thing that I have discovered is that God can fill every void! He is able to restore you to a place that it's almost as if the voids were never there.

I want for each of you reading this to know, yes it hurts and it's okay to cry. It's okay to feel it. It's okay to be angry, but don't stay there. Don't live in sadness and anger for years and years. Allow God to take it and heal your heart. You deserve it!

Pause For Reflection

What kind of relationship did you have with
your father? Do you know your father? Do you
have daddy issues? Use these next couple of
pages to write about it and then write a letter
to your dad, telling him all the things you have
never been able to say.

_____

_____

_____

_____

_____

_____

_____

_____

_____

_____

_____

_____

_____

Chapter 8

Road to Recovery and Moving Forward

With all that I have been through, situations like this will only make you bitter or better! I have chosen to be better! I want the same for you! You honestly have to choose which route you will go in. No one can make the decision for you! Ask yourself:

1. Will I be bitter or better?
2. Will I choose to be positive, or will I be negative?
3. Will I be grateful, or will I be mad about what I don't have?
4. Will I stay depressed, or will I live life to the fullest?
5. Will I allow fear to control me?
6. Will I hold on to my daddy or mommy issues?
7. Will I stay angry?

There are many people around me that I have encountered in my life that chose to stay stuck! I'm grateful that God gave me the courage I needed to tackle every area in my life to be greater.

It's important to realize that the quality of our lives is often determined by the choices we make! And our responses to the things that we didn't have control over and that's okay. Your life circumstances may not have been chosen by you, but the direction of your life can be changed and redirected.

Most people fail to acknowledge that their choices are what got them into certain situations. And for the times when it wasn't your fault it's important to remember that God is still with you and can change your life and lead you in a new direction!

The past should be used as a reference and to gain insight. Allow it to serve its purpose to keep you from feeling trapped and it should give you a desire for change.

It is very difficult to keep non-productive thoughts out of your mind, but it is possible. Sometimes we have to not be so hard on ourselves and give ourselves grace to move forward. It takes time emotionally. There is a way out! You have to let go so that you can heal! You can't grow if you won't let go! You can't heal if you don't deal!

Things have gotten better in the last five years. I have two healthy children and they are both doing well. Tiana is in the process of Ph.D. and Tyreece is a senior in High School. I have my own house which I am proud of. I am striving to have a better relationship with my mother. She has been sobering now for over two decades, she's again a homeowner, car owner and has master's degrees! I am thriving and no longer just surviving.

Once I let go of all the hurt, pain, guilt, and shame I have was able to start living. I had to make a choice to either hold on to everything or release it and start healing? The pain I endured is very real. But the choice I made to start living and thriving is even more real. You can do the same. You can be a better woman or a better man. You can be a better parent. It's a choice! I know it's hard to release things and to forgive but remember the forgiveness is for you. Don't walk around angry!

The ball is in your court.

Let all bitterness and wrath and anger, clamour and
slander be put away from you,
along with all malice.
Ephesians 4:31

As I end this chapter of my life and begin the new, I will begin to live for me.

One of the hardest lessons I had to learn in life is that blood does not mean family. So as I entered the year 2022 I decided I will create my own family and live the rest of my days as God sees fit.

Release is Important

Release stands for :

Refuge	Find refuge in God
Enough	You are enough
Life	You can have new life
Expression	Express your feelings
Anger	Let go of anger
Scars	Ask God to help you forgive
Encouragement	God is with you through it all

I am praying for you that you will never be the same after reading this book. I encourage you to work on releasing and living in your own personal life. Practice forgiveness. Ask God to come in and restore you. It will change your life!

BEHIND THE SCENES OF THE BOOK

I am not perfect now. The difference now is that I'm no longer afraid to ask for help anymore. To begin this journey I reached out to nearly 100 people asking for their help with making this dream of mine come true. Out of the nearly 100 letters, I received feedback from twelve people. Several of them may or may not be mentioned in any of the chapters above but I want them to know how much I appreciate and thank them for setting aside some time to help me. I asked for raw honesty and they gave it. I am sharing some of the people closest to me true thoughts about me.

I call it "The Best of Both Worlds." I'm telling MY truth though my eyes and also giving you the truth about me though others.

145

Letters From The Hearts Of Others

The First Letter is from My Niece Diara (my favorite great-niece's mom) lol

Auntie:

My aunt was more than an aunt to me. She was very involved in my life. I spent weekends and the summer there when I lived in Aurora. I remember I loved to go over there to be with my cousin Tiana. Later my little cousin Tyreece came, and he was the youngest in our immediate family. We spent all the holidays together and we did it BIG! My aunt was the type if you wanted to do something she made sure you saw it through even if at the end you decided not to go that route. She was the type of aunt you could talk to about anything, and she would be honest about it.(Even if you didn't like it) she would get you all the way together chile.

Everybody loved going to Auntie's house. She opened her doors for everybody. She showed me discipline and tough love. At my aunt's house we had so much fun. We used to get in the pool all day and night. It was lit at cookouts and BBQs. I remember I lied about

146

something, and she made me write "I will not lie" 2000-3000 times. I never did that again lol she shared so many memories and I'm happy to have her in my life. Ups, downs, flaws and all my Aries baby.

My Goddaughter (she was my first real life baby).

Godmom:

Growing up I remember you always coming to get me and taking me with you somewhere. I remember the apartment you had near Baltimore Ave. We used to watch the movie Grease, (which became my favorite movie), we did puzzles, danced, and I remember you let me do your hair in ballies and barrettes. You acted like it was cute. LOL. I remember your black cat being there as well. One day you asked me if I noticed anything different about you, and I stared and said no. You hugged me because you were happy that I didn't notice your braces.

I remember when you took me to Red Lobster. I ordered a burger because I didn't like seafood. One year on my birthday you took me to the store and let me pick out which mountain bike I like. I was happy.

On Christmas you always hooked me up. My favorite time is when you bought me this old navy jacket, tan timberlands, and clothes from the Gap. Speaking of that one time we went to the Gap, and I didn't want you to buy me anything because the prices were high. You bought me these hush puppy shoes, the baby doll shoes, and I remember shoes that we use to put a penny in the front. LOL

Back then you would yell all the way down the street "Lakeshia Shenae'"!! Omg lol I remember when you first bought your Chevy Malibu, and you used to drive with one leg up.

I remember you added all these extra God kids without my approval. Didn't like that. You used to take me to Tiana recitals, and drill team competitions and I used to love them!

I remember when you first bought your house, and we used to come over and swim in the pool. You were gonna make the third room a room for me, but I think Tyreece came soon after that. I remember asking you to have a baby LOL, and you let me name him Markell. When he was born, you called and laid me out for some reason I forgot lol.

I remember you being mad at me for like 5 years because I didn't listen to you or whatever LOL. I was on my phone after like 10pm and you said I couldn't, which was way too controlling for me. LOL. Also when I stopped going to school you tried to get me in another school, but I don't know what happened. I remember wanting TyReece when he was little, but you were being a pain, so I just gave up. lol

When we had a fire at my house when I was a teen, I remember the Tiffany matching necklace and bracelet set that got destroyed. You bought me that set, and I loved it.

When you gave birth I came to the house to visit you and Tyreece, and when you got the back surgery, me, my mom, and the kids came to see you. Oh yea, I remember you braiding my hair in micros and into a ponytail. I loved it. Lol. Also, that time I got in a fight with my mom's ex-husband, you came to take me and Kelise to the Motel 6.

You got mad at me for telling Martel that you got married. There are many great memories, but I will not forget that you came to see me when I graduated, and you were there for my grandmother's memorial. Always

149

remember that Naair is your "fav," so I hope to
be with him forever.

Thanks for everything
Lakeshia

Dena, my street running partner and crime.

Wan:

What can I say: We went to high school
together, however we didn't become tight until
right after your graduation. Dena and
Towanna, if you saw one, then you saw them
both! Remember when I used to drag you out
with me to EVERY occasion, party, cookout, or
drive by? Didn't matter what was going on, we
were there. Our weekdays were for work, but
BABY our weekends were for the streets, the
drive-by was all you. You have dragged me to
your "dude's" houses on numerous occasions.
And you better know I went willingly. If there
was something that peaked your intuition, you
were going to find out, and I was there for it
and you…PERIOD!
   We were together, tight, thick as thieves,
from our early twenties, mid-thirties, growing

and learning from one another. You bought your house, which encouraged me to buy my first house (thank you friend). You mothered with your whole heart and soul, I saw it myself, day after day and year after year. There is nothing you wouldn't do for Tiana and Tyreece, and you haven't changed or waivered in this area AT ALL. Supermom is who you are, just ask T&T.

As we began to grow and build our lives we always stayed connected, by phone at minimum. We would pick up and get caught up and it would feel like we hadn't missed a beat. Towanna, you are mean at times, you know this and others that know and love you know this. But I'm here to tell you today, that guess what, you should get better with that! It is NOT too late. We must intentionally work on being positive. This is for our own good, and health. Being optimistic and thinking positive takes work, and nothing worth having is easy.

Here's how I will end this, it doesn't matter if you don't talk to me, I have moved past it, I have forgiven myself and YOU ARE STILL ONE OF MY CLOSEST AND LONGEST

FRIENDS. You nor I can change that. I love you forever and ever!
   Sealed with a kiss and a tear.

Then there's Liza my aunt always pop up at your door or try to be there if you needed me. For that I will always love you. I'm not much of a writer, so I'll end this now. We miss you guys.

My adopted sister Diane Mapp wrote a letter that was too emotional for me to share I cried like a baby. We have had disagreements and fights, but she loves me, and I love and soooo proud of her. One of the STRONGEST chicks I know. I'm so glad our sister brought you into my life.

Last but not at all the least my lil/big cousin Jordy.
His is not necessarily a view of me but a memory.
He made the attempt and that's what matters to me.
Plus I don't really remember it all so Thanks
Lamar....I love you forever:

I remember you living with aunt Marilyn,
and I called myself running away from home
and cane to Aunt Marilyn's house where you
were. You had just had Tee-Tee. I remember
you hooking me up with your girlfriend and
me getting on your nerves to give me her
number then after it was over you were mad at
me claiming I mistreated her.

I remember trying to hook up with Dee, but
you weren't having it. I took you and her to
Chickie and Pete's.

A Little Note to My Mother

I personally understand the impact that trauma has on a person, especially a young person. As an adult I understand what it means to say, "I did the best I could'. I am so sorry that you had to experience all those dark days and nights.

I pray that you find peace and happiness. I love you and I forgive you. It's time to forgive yourself and LIVE YOUR LIFE.

Love,
Towanna your first born

A GLIMPSE INTO MY LIFE
THROUGH PHOTOS

All Me.

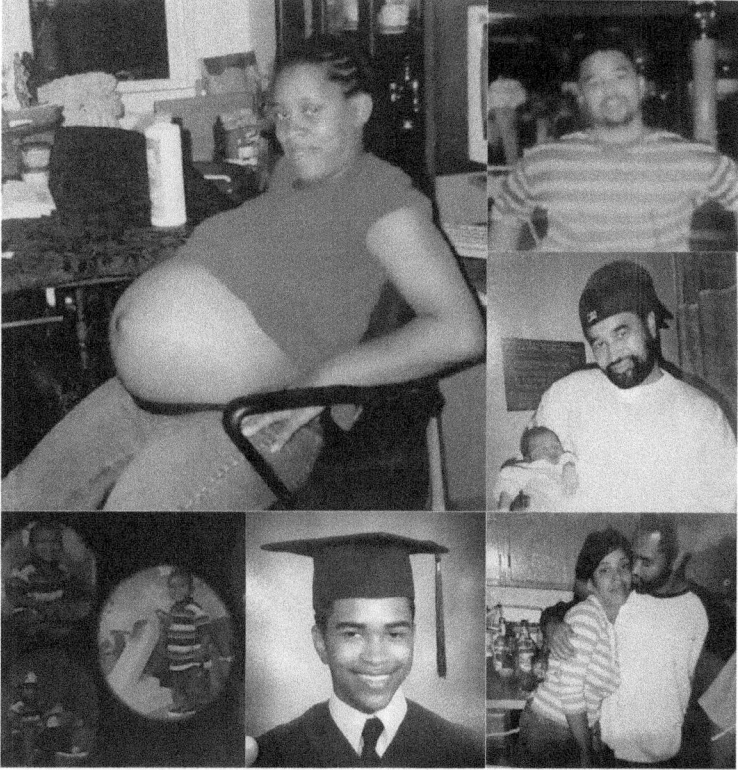

Maurice (Ty'Reece's dad) and son TyReece

My mother and Friend Angie

My godsons, Christian, Christopher, and Aaron, goddaughter
Lakeisha, husband Nasirr, and daughter Kelise and Mrs.
PeeWee (like family) in the back.

Cousins Tara and Natasha, Aunt Patricia, and brother Bravette

Paternal Grandmother Christine, my mother, Aunt Dotty,
cousins Roschell and Bernard, niece Kelly, goddaughter
Lakeisha and friend Lisa W.

Steven (Tiana's father) and Tiana

Friends: Tiana, Stephaine, Lisa W., Lisa A., Tynine, Niece
Sinamon, and son TyReece

Friend Tiana and nieces Kemaya and Sinamon

My mom, niece Diara, great-niece E'dyn, adopted sister Shai, niece Kay

My aunt Dotty, niece Diara, great-niece E'dyn, my daughter
Tiana and cousins Jordy, Ragina, and Anthony, his wife Kate,
and their children

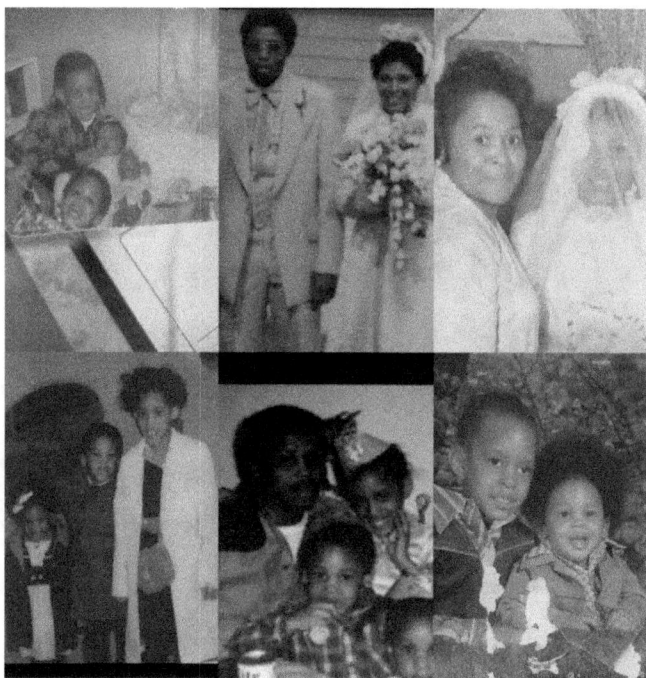

My mom, dad (Bravette) maternal grandmother (Daisy), brother(Bravette) and sister (Saron)

Maternal Grandmother (Daisy) my mother, my brother
Bravette and sister Saron

Maternal Great Grandmother, Martha, Maternal Grandmother Daisy, my mother, My Aunt Snoot, and older cousins Rosa and Liz.

My high school girlfriends D'Nae, Meatha, Michelle and Tina

My mothers, mother Daisy and father Albert, Paternal
grandparents, Christine and Furney and dad (Bravette) parents
Betty and Donald Fleet

Cousin Chanell, My dad (Bravette) my brother Bravette and my daughter Tiana

Sister Rashada and brothers Jamal and Bravette

Grandmother Christine, bother Jamal, sister Rashada, niece
Kemaya and nephew Nile

Paternal grandmother (Christine) brothers Jamal and Bravette,
brother in-law (Jose) Like a brother (Nelson) and sister
Rashada

My dad (Bravette) my brother (Bravette) my daughter (Tiana),
my son Ty'Reece and great niece E'dyn

Brother Jamal, sister Rashada, niece Kemaya, daughter Tiana, son Ty'Reece and Nephews Tyree and Nile

My stepmother (Nadine) brother (Bravette) and stepsisters
Stephaine, Tracy, and Kim

Girlfriend D'Nae

Biological father James, sister Tianna, my daughter Tiana, cousin Leatha, Aunt Leeton, brother Nate, and his 4 children

My mom, Aunt Linda (they share the same father), and my cousins Tasha, George, Sharde, and Missy

My daughters aunt Sue, Cousin Roschell, Lisa, Wanda

Maternal grandmother, my cousin Anthony, my girlfriend
D'Nae, my great-niece E'dyn, my niece Diara, my daughter
Tiana, and my sister Rashada

"As I end this chapter of my life and begin the new, I will begin to live for me."

~Towanna Pressley